"My whole life would be different if I hadn't read this book."

Elizabeth, 16

"This is a great book about how to make it in the world and stop being jealous, to be a winner, and to congratulate yourself."

Lisa, 16

"This book can make you understand your parents better."

Angela, 15

"This book will help you to be noticed by the opposite sex."

John, 16

"If everyone read this book, the world would be a much happier place."

Tracy, 15

"My brother should read this book. It would change his whole attitude."

Carol, 16

"Whoever doesn't read it will become a loser."
Harold, 15

Tonya Kc

I DARE YOU

JOYCE L. VEDRAL, Ph.D.

I DARE YOU

BALLANTINE BOOKS • NEW YORK

Library of Congress Catalog Card Number: 83-6096

ISBN 0-345-32310-6

This edition published by arrangement with Holt, Rinehart and Winston

Manufactured in the United States of America

First Ballantine Books Edition: June 1985

This book is dedicated to my father,
the late David Yellin, a man who *dared*.
And to all who want the best from life
and are willing to take a chance.

– CONTENTS –

– ACKNOWLEDGMENTS –

Without a whole school of winners behind me, I would never have been able to write this book. So I want to say thank you to Joe Vale, who naturally lives the ideas in this book. Thank you to Barbara Vale, who is never surprised by success. Thank you to Emily Bloomenstein, who is always "up." Thank you to my daughter, Marthe Simone Vedral, for her sense of humor and her intelligence. Thank you to Lee Davidson, because she said "work like crazy."

I want to say thank you to my colleagues, Dory Davidson, Joan Roberts, Irma Drosh, and Mae Allen, for their gentle encouragement. Thank you to Bernard Malamud, my mentor, for telling me that I have a way of "compelling life to work for me." Thank you to professors Roger Cayer and Mitchell Leaska for believing in me. Thank you to Jerry Braunstein for being a part of my "magic of believing." And most of all, thank you to Martha Yellin, my wonderful mother, for her steadfast confidence in me. And thank you to my father, David Yellin, although he is no longer with us, because he is the man who *dared*.

Thanks are not enough to offer to the most important people involved with this book, the students of Julia Richman High School. Without their active participation and experimentation, there would be no stories in this book. Every success story in the text is a true account of how they "worked the book." So, to my wonderful students at Julia Richman High School, thank you, thank you, thank you. And thank you to Andrew Jones, our astute principal, for putting up with a teacher who is slightly "offbeat."

Thank you, Rick Balkin, for discovering this book.

Finally, and perhaps most important, thank you to Marc Cheshire, for the intelligence and patience with which he handled this manuscript.

– INTRODUCTION –

What made me write this book? I wrote this book because in my work with young adults from the ages of fourteen through nineteen I noticed that young people seem to have a tremendous gap in their education. What is that gap? Psychology.

Yes. It seems as if no one has ever stopped to teach young adults how to use basic psychology in dealing with people. They fumble and stumble in and out of situations, getting themselves into trouble, then making it worse; getting into arguments with people over minor points and losing friends; wanting to meet people of the opposite sex so desperately, yet saying the wrong thing and alienating them. They want to make friends of the same sex, and yet they sometimes go about it in precisely the wrong way.

So I began telling my students to read books such as *Psychocybernetics, How to Win Friends and Influence People*, and *How to Be Your Own Best Friend*. While the students found these books helpful, many of the examples in the books were directed to life situations that were out of the realm of teenagers.

The next step was obvious. My students begged me to write a book so that they could have some of my "wisdom." Word got around and I began to get constant requests to write down my secrets.

In deciding what to write about, I studied the particular needs of the many teenagers I had dealt with over the years. What was it that they really needed?

Well, the answer was quite clear to me. First of all, they needed to be challenged to use their potential. They needed to be reminded that life is indeed short, but not as short for them now as it will be thirty years from now. They needed to be told that they can do whatever they want with their lives if they learn how to set goals, organize their time, and respect themselves. After they learned that, they would be ready for the second half of the book, the part that teaches them to use psychology with people in order to have a happy, successful life.

Countless young people have tried the principles in this book with astounding results. They have become happy in their seemingly hopeless family situations, they have made new friends, have gotten difficult jobs, have minimized troublesome situations, and have learned to get along with "problem" teachers. They have, in effect, "worked the book" and have come back to thank me.

I DARE YOU

1

Do You Want to Become Known?

Lots of people out there. Lots of people doing a lot of talking, but who is making anything happen? Lots of people with dreams and hopes, but who is going to see their dreams come true and their hopes realized? *You*. Now that you have this book.

This book is all about you doing exactly what you want to do with your life. Why not? You only have one. Why be a fool and say "I could have done this," or "I should have done that," when you are too old to do anything about it. Now is the time to take a shot, while you've still got the ball.

Your life is just beginning. You can still do anything you want to do. You haven't made the mistake of being in the wrong job for thirty years. You haven't let people tell you what to do with your life yet.

I Dare You. I dare you to take control of your life and make it go exactly the way you want it to go. I dare you to refuse to follow leaders, but instead to follow your own inner direction.

The first half of this book will help you to see what power you already possess. It will show you how to make a plan and follow it until you reach your goal. It will show you how to believe in yourself and respect yourself.

The second half will teach you how to deal with people so that life can become much easier. It can help you to have more friends, more fun, more money, the job you want, better marks in school, an easier time with your parents, and plenty of attention from the opposite sex. It will also tell you how to get yourself out of serious trouble quickly and efficiently.

The principles outlined in this book work. There's no end to what you can do once you understand them. There are many true accounts to prove their power.

Well, do you really want to make something of yourself? Do you want to become known? Do you want to be a winner or a loser? This book can make all the difference. The choice is yours, but nothing happens by just wishing, so keep reading. That's the way to make it happen. *I Dare You.*

2

You're It

It's too much work. I can't plan my life and make it happen. Maybe I'm just not smart enough to do it. Why do you underestimate yourself? Why do you get down on yourself so quickly? Let's think about it and change all that right now.

When it comes down to the cold, hard reality of life, you have no one but yourself. You may not be perfect, but you are, shall we say, "stuck" with who you are, so you might as well make the best of it and work with what you have.

You're a little too tall or a little too short. So what? Maybe your teeth are a bit crooked, or your hair is too frizzy. But it *is* you. It's the way you look. It's time for you to say to the world, "Listen, this is me, take it or leave it."

In order to appreciate who and what you really are, you have to take an inventory of yourself. What *do* you have going for you? What have you done that you're proud of? What are your talents? Haven't you got some special personal attributes that are worthy of celebration?

I'll tell you a few things to celebrate. For starters, and this may seem rather obvious at first, you are still young. You have your whole life in front of you. Anything can still happen. There is *time*. Next, you are a positive thinker. You are or you wouldn't be reading this book. You are, in fact, daring, ready to take a challenge. That makes you a potential winner right from the start.

But you have a lot more than that going for you. For example, who is in your corner? Is there anyone in your life who really cares about you? A mother, a father, grandparents, sisters, brothers, aunts, uncles, friends, teachers? I'll bet if you think about it, there are lots of people rooting for you, ready to help you in any way they can. The trouble is you probably never stop to think about the fact that they are there. You're really not alone. You're loved a lot more than you know. It's time to start enjoying that fact. It will make you feel stronger.

What is really different about you? I want you to think about this. There must be something that you really admire about yourself. Maybe it's your sexy eyes or your beautiful hair. Maybe it's the way you dance or the way you talk or the fact that you always seem to say the right thing. Maybe it's the way you dress or play a musical instrument, or the way you sing or make people laugh. Think about it. What makes you special?

What have you accomplished in your life so far? Have you ever counted your achievements? How many years of hard, grueling school have you gotten through? How many tests have you passed in your life? Have you been on any teams, joined any clubs? Did you ever win an award or a trophy? Were you chosen over others for something special?

Of course you've achieved many things in your life. It's time to start rejoicing about your own successes. It's time to learn to pat yourself on the back and say, "I'm the greatest." Muhammad Ali knew that secret. He called himself the greatest, and he became the greatest. He realized, as you must, that he was a pretty special person.

Whenever you achieve something, no matter how minor it is, congratulate yourself. Don't take yourself for granted. You got an 87 on a difficult social studies test. Think about it and tell yourself, "I'm terrific." Don't say, *I should have gotten a 90*, or *It was just luck*. Stop putting yourself down.

Obviously there's a big difference between recognizing success and bragging. No one likes to hear all about how great you are. In fact, what everyone wants to hear is how great they are (and this will be discussed in the second half of the book). But *you* need to hear how great you are, and you're the one to say it. You have to learn to love and appreciate yourself. It's the first step to success.

When you congratulate yourself for doing something difficult and succeeding, you reward yourself for good behavior. This reward encourages you to overcome obstacles the next time you meet them. For example, let's say you didn't feel like going to school this morning. You thought about pretending you were sick so you could stay home, and if that didn't work, you thought about simply playing hookey. But you didn't give in to that urge. You went anyway. Later in the day you thought about it and said to yourself, "I'm glad I went to school today because now I'm not behind in my work. I did the right thing and I should be proud of myself." Then the next time you're tempted to give in to laziness, you'll remember how good you felt about yourself when you overcame laziness, and you'll be inspired to succeed again. One success leads to another. It's a chain reaction. But—and here's the catch—you must learn to stop putting yourself down because of your faults and start congratulating yourself for all of your achievements.

Let other people compliment and praise you too. Have you ever found yourself putting yourself down when someone tries to give you a compliment? Someone says, "You really look great today." You say, "You must be kidding, I look terrible." Stop it. Just stop the act. You *do* look good. Accept the compliment. Just say "Thank you." By simply looking directly at the person, and with an appreciative smile saying "Thank you," you are accepting the compliment and it is registered in your subconscious mind. You are now that much more positive about yourself. By denying the compliment, you are lowering your self-image, and your subconscious mind registers you as not worthy of praise. Why deliberately work against yourself that way?

When you say, "I'm no good at sports," the next time you're asked to join a volleyball game, the words will echo in your subconscious mind, "I'm no good at sports. I can't play volleyball." Then, whenever you are asked to play, you will say, "I can't play, I'm no good." You'll miss out on all the fun. You will create a negative self-image.

If you find it necessary to speak honestly about a weakness, put it in a positive rather than a negative way. Instead of saying "I'm no good in math," say "I'd like to improve my math scores." Instead of saying "I can't dance," say "I have to work on learning some new dance steps." Remember: Be positive, positive, positive. Words have power. Your own words can encourage or defeat you. Every time you say something negative about yourself you weaken yourself. Every time you say something positive about yourself you strengthen yourself. Be your own best friend, not your own worst enemy.

Learn to stop all negative talk about yourself. If you have nothing good to say about yourself, say nothing at all. Keep your mouth shut, no matter how hard it may seem at the time. No one wants to hear your sob story anyway.

Why do people like to put themselves down? Simple. They think it gives them the right to keep doing the wrong thing, rather than trying to improve. For example, if you say that you're shy, you don't have any pressure on you to be sociable. You can hide in a corner and wait for the world to discover you, and then when the world doesn't beat a path to your door, you can blame it all on your shyness. If you say that you can't dance, then no one will bother you and you won't have to learn. Then you can feel sorry for yourself and be jealous of all those good dancers.

What are you really doing? Copping out. But where does it get you? It gets you nowhere, and you end up being angry and resentful. If you seal your fate with words, if you label yourself a failure, then the case is closed. You don't have to think about it anymore. But who are you really fooling? No one, not even yourself.

There is no need to insult yourself, anyway; there are lots of people who will be glad to do it for you. "Haven't *you* been invited to the party?" "What happened to your hair?" "You're getting fat."

What is really behind a put-down? The person putting you down may have been put down by someone else. People who have little respect for themselves put you down because they feel so small that they have to make you smaller than they are. That's all there is to it. If you realize this, put-downs will roll right off you.

Did you ever go out with someone who seemed to be trying to put you down, make you feel negative about yourself? Maybe the person implied that your clothes were not "the latest," or that you didn't speak the way he or she thought you should. Perhaps you could tell that this person did not really wish you well. Did you find yourself making excuses for yourself? If this has ever happened to you, don't let it happen again. Just stop the person cold and say, "This is me. Take it or leave it. These are *my* clothes. This is the way I talk. I may not be perfect, but it's what I have to work with and I'm proud of it." Don't ever let people put you down. Who are they to judge you, anyway? What makes them perfect?

If you tried to please everyone, you would lose your mind. There are just too many opinions out there. Whom *should* you please? Yourself, or course. But first you have to find out what you like and what you don't like, and you have to start living up to your own demands.

Here are some charts that will help you to use the information discussed in this chapter. By doing the exercises, you will apply the things you learned in the chapter to your own life-situation, and you will see your life begin to change for the better.

———————

Make a list of things you like about yourself. Remember: physical, mental, personality, talents, and abilities.

Things I have going for me
Example: I'm a good dancer.

1. I'm a good listener
2. I'm a hard worker
3. I'm honest ~~and~~ ~~straightforward~~
4. I'm a good dancer
5. I get along with ~~people~~
6. I'm young

Make a list of the things you have already achieved.

Things I have achieved
Example: I won the Math award.

1.
2. I have a ~~job~~
3.
4.

Make a list of people who are "in your corner."

1.
2. Mom
3.
4.

Make a list of compliments you have received. Think about these compliments and mentally accept them. Tell yourself that they are in fact true. Believe them.

Compliments I have received
Example: "You have beautiful eyes."

1. I love you.

2. You're so beautiful.

3. Nice legs

4. that suit is great on you

5. I love your dress

6. I love your movements

7. you're just fabulous

Think of all the times you put yourself down. Make a list. Mentally argue against the self-put-down.

Self Put-Down
Example: I said, "I'm such a slob." (Mentally argue no. I'm just careless sometimes. I have to be more alert.)

1. I have my own [illegible]

2. I'm too jealous [illegible]

3. I'm too serious [illegible]

4. I'm too obsessed w/ [illegible]

5. I should be thin [illegible]

3

What Happened?

It's Saturday night and you're home watching TV again. What happened? The summer is here and you don't have a job. What happened? It's the night of the big party and you have nothing to wear. What happened? Simple. You didn't think ahead. You didn't make a plan.

Did you ever stop to think about how amazing it is that huge skyscrapers could be erected? Think about the fact that they don't collapse, that every intricate operation was so well performed that everything fits together perfectly. That is because there was a plan. Someone thought ahead and carefully planned out what had to be done.

Your life is no different. If you want results, if you don't want things to "fall apart," you have to make a plan. Without a plan you're lost, drifting, merely passing time. But with a plan, you can aim at a target, and you will be likely to get exactly what you want out of life.

Planning is what separates the wishful thinkers from the achievers. Both groups have dreams and goals. But it is the achievers who take action and chart out specific methods to reach their goal. Achievers are winners, people who are always "working" for something. Wishful thinkers are losers. They merely wait for something to happen to them. They expect to get lucky and reach their goals without working.

Can you plan your life? Yes, in a way. The first thing you need to do is to find a place to think. Find a quiet spot where you can concentrate. This can be at home, in school, in the library—anywhere where you can be free of interruptions. Then sit in this quiet spot, with a pencil in hand, and begin to jot down your dreams, your goals in life: what you really want to do. Before you know it, you will have written down so many exciting ideas that you may think you're getting carried away with yourself. You may even say to yourself, "I'll never be able to do it all." Don't think that way even for a minute. When you finish this book, you'll be amazed by what you can do.

Your plan should be divided into three categories. The first category should include your plans for the present: today. The second category should cover your short-range goals: the things you want to do within the next few months. The third and final category should cover your long-range goals: what you want to do with your life. In other words, where you want to be ten years from now.

Let's talk about your plan for today. When you get up in the morning, think about what you're going to do with your time. You may go to school, hang around after classes, then go home and watch TV, talk on the phone for a while, eat dinner, play outside, watch some more TV, do some homework, and then go to sleep. But what if you made a plan? Would things be different?

What if you made a list of everything you wanted to accomplish that day? For example, you might remind yourself to see someone about an after-school job, to speak to the baseball coach about joining the team, to stop by the sporting goods store to get a jacket, or to call a friend for a date Saturday night.

Suppose you did that? Suppose you thought about all the things you wanted to accomplish that day and wrote them all down? You know what? You would probably do them. There's something strange about making a list. You tend to want to accomplish what you have written down because you know you will get a good feeling when you check off each item. As you check things off, you gain confidence in yourself and it spurs you on to do the other things on the list.

Think of what would happen if you made a list every day. You would accomplish those things that you're always forgetting to do but really want to do.

Once you learn to plan on a day-to-day basis, planning for a short-range goal becomes easy. Suppose you want to get your body in shape so that you can qualify for the track team or so that you will look good on the beach this summer. With planning, you can probably accomplish this goal.

How can you do it? Analyze the situation and think about what steps have to be taken to accomplish the goal. Then include the steps into your daily plan, which, when added up, will result in a three-month plan.

Here's how it works. Suppose you're thinking about joining the track team. You don't just talk about it, you do it. When you make out your daily plan you could decide to get up an hour earlier each morning so that you could exercise and run. Why put yourself through all this "aggravation"? The answer is obvious. If you are serious, you know that no one else can do it for you. If you want to make that team, to be in shape, you and only you must make the move and pull your lazy body out of bed an hour early every morning. When you think about the prize you will be getting, you won't mind paying the price. What makes it easier for you to pay the price is your plan. It is written down, so you say to yourself, "It must be done."

It works the same way with every goal you have. If you want to look good at the beach, you must face the fact that you will have to exercise every day, not just when the mood hits you. Every morning, you should do your sit-ups, push-ups, and leg raises. You shouldn't become discouraged because you don't see results the first week. If you keep at it, you will eventually see the results. Soon it becomes habit, just like brushing your teeth in the morning. A plan can do all this. It can make certain things become automatic.

Whether you want to become a better dancer, to get your schoolwork done ahead of time, or to improve your vocabulary, you can achieve your goals by incorporating them into your daily plan.

You see how a daily plan can work, and how it can lead to short-range goals that take a few months to accomplish, but how can a daily plan eventually affect what you do with your life? Suppose, for example, you want to become a secretary or a psychologist, or a professional pianist, or a diamond cutter. What exactly can you do?

If you want to become a secretary, you would take whatever business courses are offered in school. You would write down in your daily plan to see the guidance counselor about career opportunities in the business world. You would then write into your daily plans some library work and then some reading about the business world. You might join the secretarial club. You would do some research on what business courses are available for post-high-school study.

If you want to become a professional pianist, you would schedule into your daily routine some time for practice. You would also do some research as to where to find the best private tutoring in piano. You might also speak to the student in the school orchestra who plays the piano.

Get the picture? Your long-range goal will never materialize unless you take small simple steps, steps written into your daily plan. These small steps accumulate and eventually provide a staircase that takes you directly to your goal.

But my goal will take too long, you might say. Ten years. You can't wait that long. I have news for you. You'll be passing those ten years anyway. The difference is that with a goal and a plan to achieve that goal, you'll be making progress during those ten years, while if you had no goal, in ten years you'd be in the same position you are now, only ten years older. So what's it going to be? Ten years from now will you be a drifter, someone looking around for something to happen by magic, or will you have accomplished a well-planned objective? You can always be a delivery boy or a drive-in waitress in ten years if nothing better comes along, and that may happen if you don't have a game plan.

But this doesn't have to happen to you if you take action now. Why become a businessman when you want to be a college professor? Why become a secretary when you want to be a dancer? Why become a lawyer when you want to be a carpenter? Do what you *really* want to do.

It's time to get past the childhood game of "What do you

want to be when you grow up?" and start turning those wishes, those dreams, into realities. Plans can make this happen because they take you to your goal in small steps. As the saying goes, A journey of a thousand miles begins with one step.

"But I'm afraid. What if I don't succeed?" That's what people love to say. Well, so what? What did you lose? At least you tried doing something you really wanted to do.

I did. I climbed to the top of Mount Kenya in East Africa. The climb took three days and the altitude went up to 17,500 feet. What if I had gotten mountain sickness? What if I had fallen? What if I had been attacked by a wild animal? I might have been killed. What if, what if, what if. If I thought about all the "what if's" I would never have made the trip. Come to think about it, if you keep asking yourself "what if," you may never get out of bed in the morning. What if you slip on the bathroom floor? What if you miss the bus? What if you get mugged? Forget the "what if's." Just do what you need to do. I did. I put one foot in front of the other and I kept climbing. There were times when I didn't think I would make it. But I just kept telling myself, "One more step. Just one more step."

What happens when you make a mistake in your planning, and you find yourself going in the wrong direction? Change the plan. It's better to waste only two years going in the wrong direction than to waste the rest of your life.

I know a man who was a policeman for six years. One day he decided he hated being a cop and that he really wanted to be a doctor. You know what he did? He applied to medical school. He is now a doctor. He may have been a little old to enter medical school, but he's a doctor. Why? He realized that he had only one life and he decided to take a shot at what he really wanted. You have that right too. Isn't it better to pay the price of backtracking, of moving in another direction, then to spend the rest of your life bored and unhappy?

So what if you take business courses in high school and then realize that you really want to become a teacher and not a secretary? You can still apply to a teaching college by taking the necessary courses in evening high school. Why not? What's stopping you? Just because you made a mistake doesn't mean you can't correct it by backtracking. Remember: It's never too late—never.

Maybe you don't really know what you want to do when you graduate from high school. You're not alone. Give yourself time. Talk to people. Speak to your guidance counselor. Go to the library and get books about careers that interest you. Ask the librarian to help you. Talk to people in professions that interest you. Ask your teachers to put you in touch with doctors, lawyers, accountants, etc. Get an idea what these professions are all about from people who are actually practicing them. Talk to auto mechanics at the local garage. Start a conversation with the local grocery-store owner or the camera-shop owner. Look around. Begin to think seriously about how you want to fit into the world. Imagine yourself in various jobs. Think about how you would feel. The results may be surprising. Soon you will sense what is and what is not for you. Can you picture yourself being a waiter or a waitress, a bus driver, a social worker? Soon you will get an idea of what really pleases you. This search is worth your time because you may spend the rest of your life in that career.

"Okay. So I do the research and I make a plan," you say. "But what about all the people who try to tell me what to do with my life? Parents, friends, and relatives are always giving me advice, offering opinions and trying to do my thinking for me. What should I do?"

Parents love their children so much that sometimes they

try to do too much for them. They want them to succeed, and once in a while they exert a little too much pressure on their children to head in a certain direction. They mean well, but they can forget that there may be something inside of you that they haven't yet realized. So it is up to you to help them to understand that within you is a talent so special that it must be pursued. You can't merely "follow in Dad's footsteps," not unless you want what Dad does.

At times, doing what you really want to do may cause problems with your parents. I once met a young man who is now a well-known chef. His father wanted him to work in the family oil business, but he chose to go his own way. At first his father was furious. Now his father helps him give banquets, and is very proud of him. Parents very often come around. But don't be afraid to listen to them. They have some good advice too. You'll find this out more and more as time goes on. In the long run your parents can't live your life, so stop worrying that they will make you into what you don't want to be. *Only you can make that mistake.*

I remember how people reacted to my idea to write a book. They told me about all the poor writers struggling to get published. They reminded me of all the time and energy I might be wasting. But I didn't listen to them. I just forged ahead.

Thousands of books get published every year, I thought, so why not mine? So I wrote my first book and sent it out to various publishers, and guess what? I was published and I use it in my English classes. I'm glad I didn't listen to the negative thinkers, the jealous bystanders, the ones who were so concerned that I was wasting my time.

Sometimes there will be a legitimate reason for not achieving a goal. Other times you will have to admit that you did not achieve your goal because you were too lazy to invest the necessary time. Finally, there are goals that you will realize were unrealistic to begin with. They simply prove to be too difficult. There is no crime in admitting to yourself that the goal is not for you and finding another more achievable goal.

Here are some charts that will help you to use the information discussed in this chapter. By doing the exercises, you will apply the things you learned in the chapter to your own life-situation, and you will see your life begin to change for the better.

Make a plan for your day. Do this the night before or early in the morning.

Plan for the Day
Example: Get an employment form from the guidance office.

1.

2.

3.

4.

Make a list of your short-range goals (goals that can be accomplished within a few months).

Short-range goals
Example: Save up for a new stereo.

1.

2.

3.

4.

Make a list of your long-range goals (goals that may take a few years or more).

Long-range goals
Example: Become a lawyer.

1.

2.

3.

4.

4

Call the Police

You have so many ideas and plans. How can you possibly accomplish everything? You may as well give up, right? Of course not. You just have to get organized.

If you could control your time, you would have control of your life. Think about it. What is your life really made up of? Time. What do you do with your time? Why is it that some people seem to get so much more done than other people? Do they have more hours in the day? Obviously not. They have learned the secret of controlling time. You can accomplish all the goals you create for yourself if you just learn to manage your time properly.

What do you do with your time? There are 168 hours in a week. Think about it. One hundred sixty-eight hours of time on your hands.

Obviously some things must be done in order to live. Sleeping, eating, and basic hygiene will use up 11 hours a day, or 77 hours a week, if you allow 8 hours for sleeping, 2 for eating and 1 for hygiene. Now you have 91 hours left. You go to school for about 5 hours a day and you use up 1½ hours traveling. All that takes 32½ hours. You have 58½ hours left. To round it out, let's say you have 50 hours left to yourself each week. Fifty hours of free time. What do you do with it?

You could spend most of your 50 hours as a spectator, watching. Observing. Looking on. You could sit in front of the TV and see things rather than do things. Or you could sit in movie houses and fantasize. Yes, and you can live your life watching other people, and just let your own life slip away. Call the police. Don't let it happen.

As for the winners, they're bored with TV, and they're too jealous to watch it for long—all those people on that screen having fun while they just sit watching it happen. No way. They want to be out there making things happen. Don't you? No one ever came out of that TV and asked you to dance. So I guess you'd better get out there and see what you can stir up in the real world.

Don't misunderstand. There are some valuable aspects to television. You can, for example, use it to relax for an hour after a hard day. You may want to watch a special movie, or see a certain show for a particular reason. That's fine. But remember your priorities for spending your time.

What else can you do with your time? Well, first of all, you'll want to relax, maybe even be lazy. Take one hour a day for that. That's enough. Now you have 43 hours left in the week. You're young and full of life and you want to have fun. Say you have 10 hours a week to play. Now you have 33 left. You can work to earn extra money during that 33 hours, or you can decide to use the time for something that is important to you like swimming, reading, taking photographs, or making your own clothes.

The most important thing is to decide on your priorities. What is more important to you at this point in your life, getting new clothes (which you can buy if you work during your 33 free hours) or participating in the swimming team so that you can try out for the Olympic Games? Think about it for a moment. Which use of time will give you more personal satisfaction, more pleasure? Since there is a limited amount of time, you will have to begin making choices about how to use it.

Your thinking may go as follows: "If I work, I can buy beautiful clothes and then I will feel better when I go to school and to parties. I'll be more attractive. But on the other hand, if I join the swimming team, I will feel good about myself. I'll have that sensation of being special and I'll feel more confident. That alone will get me more attention from the opposite sex, and at the same time I'll be doing something that I really want to do." Or, your reasoning may go in the opposite direction. "If I work I can buy beautiful clothes and get more attention from the opposite sex, but if I join the swimming team, not only will I not be able to work and buy clothes, but I'll probably be dragging myself around, tired from all that swimming. On top of that I won't have the money I need."

Being honest with yourself, thinking carefully about your choices, will help you to make honest decisions about using your time.

Your use of time will not be a problem once you have planned your goals. If, for example, you have decided to join the track team to get your body in shape, you will obviously have to spend about an hour a day exercising. If you want to get a term paper finished on time (and who doesn't), you'll want to schedule that into your weekly plan.

If you want to improve your reading or investigate something that interests you, you'll want to plan some weekly reading time. You will arrange your time to accomplish whatever you have determined you must do in order to achieve your goals.

Too much work? Too much of a hassle? Then don't do it. But then don't complain when nothing happens. No one cares more about yourself than you do. Always keep that in mind. If you don't make anything happen for yourself, probably no one else will. People can help you by encouraging you from time to time or by giving you advice, but in the long run, it's all up to you.

"But there just isn't enough time," you say. Well, let's see what you can do with the time you do have. Efficient use of time will help you to get so much done that people will wonder how you do it. For example, if you set aside two hours a day to write, you could write a book in less than a year.

To use your time wisely you need to set priorities. Once you know what is most important to you, you can learn to cut corners. Maybe you're sleeping more than you should be. Perhaps you're wasting a lot of time and you don't even realize it. For example, you could learn to use time on the bus or subway. You could read while you are traveling to school. By doing two things at once, you increase your available time. Most people just look around and stare into space on buses and subways. "But," you say, "I can't concentrate on the bus. There's too much noise." Stop making excuses. If you were really motivated, there would be no problem. As the old saying goes, Where there's a will, there's a way. I add, If there's no will, then there is no way.

Anything is possible. I'll demonstrate the point. Suppose someone offered to give you a thousand dollars to read ten pages during the half-hour bus ride to school. All you would have to do is read the material and answer a few simple questions about the reading. Do you think you could manage to block out all the noise, to cut off the distractions, and to focus on the text? You most certainly would. You'd be motivated. That thousand dollars would change your whole attitude about reading on the bus.

You see what I mean. If you really care about your life, if you really want to do something, you can overcome all kinds of obstacles.

Think about this. If you read 5 hours a week on the bus, in a year's time you will have read for 260 hours. I'll even give you a break. Suppose some days you don't read. You could still read for at least 150 hours more during the year. This reading could help you in many ways. You could increase your knowledge, pursue your hobbies, and increase your vocabulary and reading level.

Here are some charts that will help you to use the information discussed in this chapter. By doing the exercises, you will apply the things you learned in the chapter to your own life-situation, and you will see your life begin to change for the better.

———————————————

Divide your 168 hours a week up into time blocks by breaking it down into specifics.

My week
Sample: Sleep: 56 hours.

1. Sleep

2. Eat

3. Personal Hygiene

4. School

5. Travel to and from places

6. Relaxation

7. Party

8. Study and Homework

9. Exercise

10. Work

11. Television

12. Telephone

13. Reading

14.

15.

Use this chart to make sure you are not wasting time.

Make a list of things you would like to do but can't fit into your day.

What I would like to do
Example: Learn to play Tennis.

1.

2.

3.

4.

Review your weekly hour chart and find things that "waste time." Make a list.

Things that waste my time
Example: Too many hours watching television.

1.

2.

3.

4.

Change your wasted time into time used well. Make a list of what you did.

Changes I made
Example: Stopped watching four hours of TV a night and limited it to two. I read for one hour a night and exercised for the other.

1.

2.

3.

4.

5

I'm a Victim

You've set your goals, you have organized your time, and you know what you're going to do and when you're going to do it. But you still don't do it. Why not? You're a victim.

"I couldn't help it," you say. What you should say is, "I wouldn't help it." You wouldn't help yourself, so you just let it happen. In almost every situation, when you allow something to happen that in your heart you really don't want to happen, you can stop it. When you don't stop it, you become a victim. The dictionary definition of "victim" is someone who is tricked or duped. Why do people often allow themselves to become victims? Why are they afraid to stand up and say, "No. I will not let this happen?" You will find out the answers to these questions by the end of this chapter.

How can you stop being a victim? By getting control of your mind. Your mind, after all, rules your actions.

Are you the victim of your moods? For example, did you ever plan to do something after school, perhaps go for a job interview, and then decide at the last minute not to go because you just weren't "in the mood"? Maybe you rationalized your decision by telling yourself you would go another day, that you were not in the "right mood" that day. So you gave in to your mood and did the easy, lazy thing. You went home. Think of how you felt that evening when you reviewed the events of the day. Probably not too happy. How would you have felt if you had gone to the interview and landed the job? You would have been flying high.

What effect does giving in to your mood have on your life? Well, every time you give in to a mood, you lose a battle. In a sense, you're defeated. You are lowered in your own eyes, and you begin to think of yourself as someone who "can't help it." The next time you try to do something you've planned to do, it becomes even more difficult because you remember the last defeat. A nagging voice in your mind says, "Forget it, you can't do that. The last time you tried you were defeated." You will most likely give in again. Before you know it, you accept defeat without even trying. You begin to think of yourself as a loser. You say, "I'm a victim." But think of the effect if you overcome the difficulty and conquer your mood, if you complete the job at hand in spite of your mood. The next time you'll have confidence in yourself because you'll remember how you won the last battle.

We all have fears about trying new things. We all experience a lack of confidence, nervousness, and doubts. Learn to go past all of that. Learn to *win*.

What can we do about moods that make us victims? There

are some basic steps that can help you to gain control of your own mind.

First of all you have to learn to precondition yourself. You have to think about things before they happen. You have to imagine yourself behaving exactly the way you want to behave. Here's how it works.

Let's say you have arranged a job interview for yourself. Instead of imagining yourself being lazy and tired at the end of the day and giving in to that mood and just taking the bus home, imagine yourself getting a sudden surge of energy when you think about how important it is for you to get that job. Then imagine yourself overcoming your laziness and hopping on the bus or train and going to that interview. If you do this, chances are you will not give in to your "mood" and you will show up for the planned interview. You will feel good about yourself. You will not be a victim.

Chances are that you already precondition yourself without being aware of it, but you may be preconditioning yourself for failure. For example, perhaps you've said to yourself, "When I get home, I know my mother is going to start talking about cleaning up my room and we are going to get into an argument." Sure enough, when you get home, your mother mentions your room and you start making excuses. Before you know it you've created another "scene" with her. You created the negative scene you had imagined in your mind. But think about this. All you have to do is change what you are imagining before the event, and things may go differently. Let's say you imagine your mother talking to you about your messy room. Now you form a picture of yourself calmly agreeing with her, and you see yourself going in your room to straighten it up. Amazingly, when you go home, instead of getting aggravated when your mother mentions your room, you calmly agree and then proceed to clean it up.

Preconditioning works especially well when you want to form new habits or break old habits. Suppose your goal is to get up an hour earlier every morning in order to exercise. Despite all good intentions, every time the alarm rings at that early, dark hour, you're tired and you reset the alarm. Chances are that you have preconditioned yourself. The night before, you may have imagined the alarm ringing and saw yourself turning it forward an hour. You imagined yourself too sleepy to get out of bed. Try a different picture. Imagine yourself getting up when the alarm rings and think about how beautiful you are going to look as your body changes with the exercise. Imagine yourself feeling a sudden surge of energy and jumping out of bed and starting the exercise before you have a chance to make excuses. Replace your negative thoughts with positive thoughts. You know what? You'll have a much better chance of getting out of bed and exercising.

Don't be discouraged if you fail at first. Old habits are hard to break. If you keep at it, however, preconditioning works, and you will find that you are no longer the victim of your momentary moods.

Suppose you want to break the habit of leaving your room a mess. You know that the sight of a messy room depresses you. You know that it is impossible to find things when everything is strewn around. You want to keep your room clean, but for some reason you just keep throwing things around and contributing to the confusion. What's wrong with you anyway? Why are you doing what you don't want to do? Why are you working against yourself? You do this because you have already brainwashed yourself to believe that "you can't help it." You've always been sloppy, so you tell yourself you always will be. Perhaps your parents helped to reinforce this image. "You'll never change," they said. "You'll always be a slob." So there you are: a slob. But wait a minute. Why not change the picture? Create a new image of yourself. First straighten up your room. Then put a new idea into your mind. Imagine yourself overcoming the temptation to be sloppy. Before you know it you will have conquered the whole problem.

Preconditioning can also help at social events. You have a choice. You can precondition yourself to have a miserable time or a good time. Here's how it works. While you're getting dressed for the party you can allow negative thoughts to enter your mind. You can look in the mirror and start finding fault with yourself. You can say, "I have acne," or "What an ugly nose I have," or "I'm too fat," and finally, "I look horrible. No one will talk to me at the party." Then you go to the party and you behave strangely. You hide in the corner, thinking about how ugly you are. When someone looks at you, you quickly look away, avoiding the person's eyes. Before you know it, people *do* begin avoiding you. Why? Because you gave off negative vibes. Your body language said, "Stay away. Something is wrong with me." People pick up the message and go the other way.

What's the other choice? Positive thinking. As you're getting dressed for the party, begin to psych yourself. Put on your favorite music. Think about all the new people you are going to meet. Wear something you know you look good in. If you don't like the way you look in what you first put on, change the outfit. By leaving on an outfit you don't like, you're planning to fail. Plan to succeed. Expect the best and get it. Ralph Waldo Emerson, the well-known poet and thinker, once said, "Beware of what you want, for you *will* get it." Remember that. If you want to lose and be rejected, chances are that it will happen. If you want to win and be accepted, you will probably win and be accepted.

Imagine success. Think of the event and imagine yourself being successful. Think positively.

Studies have shown that mental discipline helps professional basketball players to improve their skills. When they imagine themselves shooting the ball into the basket, their actual ability to sink baskets improves.*

It works in other situations. Imagine yourself at a job interview, smiling, confident, saying the right things. Imagine the interviewer smiling back at you and liking you. Start to believe that people are *for* you rather than *against* you. Instead of worrying—believe.

What is worry, actually? It is imagining that the thing you fear will happen. It is seeing a "movie" of an event ahead of time—a failure movie. When you do this, you prepare for failure. You need to run a different movie through your mind before an important event, a success movie. If you do this, your chances of succeeding will be much greater.

Sometimes we find ourselves acting like victims in spontaneous situations. It happens so fast we don't even realize what happened until after the fact, when we find ourselves depressed. For example, let's say you are planning to go to a party with a date. When you meet the person, he or she says, "There's a great movie playing. I don't want to miss it. I'm not really in the mood for a party, are you? Let's forget about the party and go to the movie." And although you really are in the mood for a party, and *not* in the mood for a movie, you say, "Okay, let's go to the movie."

Why did you let yourself be "had" that way? Why didn't you speak up and express your true feelings? Were you afraid your date would reject you? What would have really happened if you had spoken up? You would have talked it

*Maxwell Maltz, M.D., F.I.C.S., *Psychocybernetics* (New York: Pocket Books, 1960).

out and would have made a compromise. But most importantly, you would have felt better about yourself. No one likes to be controlled. When you don't speak up, you are allowing yourself to be controlled.

If you think about it, you'll realize that most of the time you don't speak up only because you are afraid that you will look stupid or be rejected. But here's how to overcome that fear. Just remember that other people have the same fears that you have. They are also worried about looking stupid and being rejected. You have just as much right to express your feelings as they do. Would you reject them because they expressed their opinion? No.

Would you laugh at them or think they were stupid? No. They won't reject you either. If you speak up you will feel better about yourself.

But what happens when you do everything right and you still fail? In spite of everything, all your positive thinking, all your careful planning, you fail. So what? That just proves you're human. If you never fail you would be put on display for all the world to see: "The person who has never failed." Failure is natural. It doesn't make you a bad person. If you made an honest effort, give yourself credit for trying. Say to yourself, "I tried my best."

I'll never forget the time I participated in the Empire State Games (the New York State Olympics) as a white belt in judo. I had to fight a black belt, who had twelve years' experience. I had only been playing judo for six months but I believed I could defeat her. Well, in a short time she pinned me to the mat. I couldn't move. I felt like fainting. I was lucky to get up and take my bow. In fact, I had to climb up by holding on to the umpire's leg. But I was satisfied because I knew I had done my best. I said to myself, "I tried." And instead of losing respect for myself, I gained more respect.

So when you fail, don't be so hard on yourself; give

yourself a break. Failure is a necessary prerequisite to success. A year and a half later, I pinned a girl to the mat in a promotion contest and got my brown belt in judo.

A common reason for feeling like a failure is when your boyfriend or girl friend breaks up with you. Perhaps he or she found someone new. Think of it this way. Didn't you ever break up with someone? Did that mean that the person was totally worthless? Everyone at one time or another moves out of a relationship; it's not a mark against you.

There are hundreds of people all around you, fat, skinny, short, tall, ugly, beautiful. They come in all sizes and shapes. Nevertheless, most people find someone who thinks they're great. There is someone for each of us. That's the wonderful part of life.

So accept failure. Let yourself be sad about failure but then get mad. Get furious. Get so angry that you turn that failure into energy, and turn that energy into success. If you fail a test in school then get furious enough to stay home a few nights a week and study hard enough to get an A. Your boyfriend or girl friend left you? Sulk awhile, then go out and make new friends.

If you think about it, you'll see that anger can be transformed into energy. When you have an argument with someone, you could kick a chair, throw rocks, tear out the phone, pick on your younger brother, or spend all day talking about it. Or you can try to calm yourself down by learning to channel your anger into positive action. Take your anger, which is negative, and focus it on a positive goal.

Here are some charts that will help you to use the information discussed in this chapter. By doing the exercises, you will apply the things you learned in the chapter to your own life-situation, and you will see your life begin to change for the better.

Make a list of things that you put off because you are "not in the mood."

Things I put off
Example: Doing my sit-ups in the morning.

1.

2.

3.

4.

5.

Answer each item with a description of the way you will feel later in the day if you resist the mood and refuse to become a "victim."

Positive results of overcoming mood
Example: I will feel great when I remember that I did my sit-ups, and I will feel strong and think of how great I'll look this summer.

1.

2.

3.

4.

5.

Precondition yourself for success. Make a list of your goals, your excuses, and your counter-thoughts.

Desired Goal	Excuse	Counter-Thought
Example: Stop Smoking.	I'm Addicted.	I'm not going to be a victim. Think how I'll feel when I beat this—better wind, etc.
1.		
2.		
3.		
4.		
5.		

Use the following worksheet to keep a going record of when you turn negative energy into positive energy.

Negative event	Potential negative reaction	Positive alternative
Example: Failed the math test.	Rip up the math book.	Take a long walk, then call a friend who is good in math to ask about tutoring.
1.		
2.		
3.		
4.		
5.		
6.		

6

I'm Scared

Did you ever do something that made you lose respect for yourself? Did you ever look in the mirror and get a feeling of disgust, and say to yourself, "How could I be so stupid?" Why do people do things that in the long run make them seem smaller in their own eyes?

For one thing, many people do not really know what they believe in, what they think is right and wrong. They are "scared" to find out, so they just flounder about, hit and miss, doing whatever their immediate whim tells them to do. Then they pay the consequences of frequent loss of self-respect. The end result of this lowered self-image is an inability to succeed in life, because the person doesn't believe that he or she is worthy of success.

Don't let this happen to you. Now is the time, early in

life, to discover your values, what you and you alone believe is right and wrong. It really isn't that difficult. Stop and ask yourself the question: What is it that makes me feel disgusted with myself?

I asked a group of high school students this question. They were allowed to be anonymous. Here are some of the answers they wrote down:

When I get nasty with my mother and tell her off.
When I say yes when I want to say no.
When I'm mean to my little brother.
When I give my word to someone
    and I don't keep it.
When I curse someone out just for some little thing.
When I fail a test because I didn't study.
When I use someone.
When I don't follow through on what I planned.

The question arises, "Why not just stop doing these things, if they make you lose respect for yourself?" After all, what's more important, to give in to a momentary urge, or to be able to look in the mirror and say to yourself, "I'm beautiful. I'm a good person. I love myself"? Many times people continue doing things that make them lose respect for themselves because they are unaware that these things are eroding their self-respect. They don't stop to analyze what they are thinking. All they know is that they feel unhappy. But the corrosive effect does not go away. And each time people do something to make them lose respect for themselves, they become less and less likely to succeed in their goals in life.

So how can you stop doing what makes you lose respect for yourself? Well, the first thing is to get a clear picture of how these things make you feel about yourself. I asked some high school students how they feel when they do something wrong. Here are some of their comments:

I felt cheap and dirty.
I wished I could hide from the world.
I thought everyone knew. I didn't want to look at anyone.
I wanted to kill myself.
I was scared and confused.
I felt alone, like I didn't have a friend in the world.

I also asked my students what makes them feel good about themselves.

When I fulfill my responsibilities.
When I succeed in something I've worked hard for.
When I help someone whom no one else will help.
When I am honest with my boyfriend.

I then asked the students to tell how they felt about themselves when they resisted doing the wrong thing.

I felt strong.
I liked myself.
I kissed my hand and smiled at myself in the mirror.
I had a warm feeling inside.
I felt like I was flying.
I was smiling from ear to ear. Everyone kept asking me what happened.

Which way would you rather feel about yourself? Which way is more conducive to succeeding in life?

"But how do I find out what I really believe in?" you ask. "How can I know what my values really are?" It's really not that complicated. You do the same thing I asked my students to do. Sit down with pencil in hand and make two lists: one of everything you do that makes you feel disgusted with yourself, and one with everything you do that makes you feel good about yourself. Your own lists will tell you what you really believe in.

If you could conquer this area and begin living up to your own beliefs, you would be well on your way to success. You believe it's wrong to cheat yet you find yourself cheating. Now, at least, you can admit to yourself that you believe it's wrong and you can work on correcting yourself. If you can begin living up to your own values, you will become stronger because you will not be weakened by a guilty conscience. Studies have been made on people who do not succeed in life, and they show that these people usually suffer from a guilty conscience. They bring punishment upon themselves without even realizing that they are doing it.*

As a matter of fact, Abraham Maslow, a well-known psychologist, points out that everything we do that we believe is wrong is recorded in our subconscious mind as clearly as if a score were being kept. He says it is as if an indictment is written against us, and that that indictment serves to weigh us down. He also says that every time we do something that we really believe in, that is also recorded. So depending upon whether or not we live up to our moral values, we have either a clear conscience or a guilty conscience.†

Many of us are suffering from false guilt, guilt that we feel not because we have violated our own values, but because we failed to live up to someone else's values. Those who carry false guilt have never stopped to ask themselves the question: "Do I agree or disagree with this value?" For

*Franz G. Alexander, M.D., and Hugo Staub, *The Criminal, the Judge and the Public* (Glencoe, Ill.: Falcon Wing Press, 1956), p. 40.
†Abraham Maslow, *Toward a Psychology of Being* (New York: Van Nostrand Reinhold, 1968), p. 5.

example, suppose your mother always said "Cursing is wrong." Well, sooner or later you're going to have to ask yourself whether or not in your innermost being you agree or disagree with her. You may well agree. In fact, you may be surprised to find that most of the time you agree with the values put forth by your parents. The famous writer and religious thinker C. S. Lewis once made a study of the great religions and analyzed them to find out what most people feel is right and what is wrong. He came up with the same things my students said were right and wrong: It is right to help people, to fulfill responsibility, to be honest, to respect other people's property, and to care for the family. It is wrong to be cruel to people who are less fortunate, to shirk responsibility, to be dishonest, and to disrespect other people's property.*

There will be times, however, when you do not agree with the values put forth by others. When this happens, you have to take one of the biggest steps of maturity. You have to say to yourself, "Okay, that's his or her value or belief, but I don't agree. It doesn't mean that he or she is wrong, it just means that I don't agree with that particular value, and I don't have to feel obligated to live up to it."

Once you begin to think for yourself, honestly, about what other people say is right and wrong, you will be relieved of a lot of confusion and false guilt. It isn't easy, but unless you begin working on it now and work on it regularly, you will be paralyzed by guilt.

*Susan Scheaffer Macaulay, *How to Be Your Own Selfish Pig* (Elgin, Ill.: David C. Cook, 1982), p. 51.

Here are some charts that will help you to use the information discussed in this chapter. By doing the exercises, you will apply the things you learned in the chapter to your own life-situation, and you will see your life begin to change for the better.

———————

Make a list of things that make you feel bad about yourself, things that cause you to lose respect for yourself. Tell how you feel.

Things that cause me to lose respect for myself	*How I feel*
Example: When I am disrespectful to my mother.	Guilty and very sad.
1.	
2.	
3.	
4.	

Make a list of things that make you feel good about yourself, things that cause you to gain respect for yourself. Tell how you feel.

Things that cause me to gain respect for myself	*How I feel*
Example: When I help someone who is blind to cross the street.	Proud and happy.
1.	
2.	
3.	
4.	

Make a list of what you believe to be right and wrong. Write your own personal "Ten Commandments." It is all right if they are already in the Bible.

My Ten Commandments
Example: It is wrong to be cruel to my little brother, so: Being mean is wrong.

1.

2.

3.

4.

5.

6.

7.

8.

9.

10.

7

What's Your Name?

Names are important. Your name singles you out from all the rest. It transforms you into an individual. That's why people love to hear their names called out for everyone to hear. Your name, your beautiful name—it's you.

What if no one ever called out your name? Suppose people just pointed to you and said, "Hey, you, the one with the blue shirt." You'd probably feel angry and then isolated, like part of a vast insignificant multitude.

But think of this. How do you feel when someone you met only once remembers your name? Don't you feel flattered and surprised, and even important? You must have made some impression on that person. What is your opinion of someone like this? You probably like and respect him. The reason is simple. He liked and respected you by honoring you properly and remembering your name.

If you want people to like and respect you, remember their names. Think of it in the reverse. How do you feel about people who constantly forget your name or mispronounce it? You feel as if they are careless and that they don't think you're important enough to remember. Even if you don't think this on a conscious level, you do think it deep down inside. In effect, you reject people because you feel that they have rejected you. True, they can do something to regain your confidence, but they have to work on it.

So why set obstacles in your way from the beginning by forgetting people's names? Why not clear a pathway to being liked and respected by making a concentrated effort to remember the name of every person you meet?

How can you remember names? It's not so difficult. First of all, you have to want to remember; that is half the battle. Once you believe it is important to remember a name, you will have much less trouble doing so.

You can also try some memory tricks. Say for example the person's name is Maria. Maybe you could think of a song about Maria, and say to yourself, "When I see her again, I'll think of the song." There are many clever tricks you can use to help you remember. For some examples, see *The Memory Book* by Harry Lorayne and Jerry Lucas.

Sometimes you are introduced to a friend of a friend. The first thing you are told about the person is his or her name. Very often you aren't really listening because you are so caught up in meeting the person. So you may not even really *hear* the name to begin with. This means trouble right away because the moment you want to direct something to that person's attention, you have to say, "I'm sorry, what did you say your name is?" You can avoid this situation by making a point to pay full attention when you are introduced in the first place. Repeat the names immediately. The person says, "Joyce, I'd like you to meet Jackie." You should say, "Hi, Jackie. I'm glad to meet you." By deliberately repeating the name it will be easier to remember.

Some young people I know decided to see how remembering people's names would affect their lives. Here are some of the results.

Jesus, whose name is difficult to forget, had this amusing experience:

One day my best friend's cousin came to Spanish Harlem where I live. But my best friend's cousin has a strange name, at least for our neighborhood it's strange. Eugene. Most of my friends forgot his name and just said to him, "What's up, 'rican?" (That's what we call a person if we can't remember their name.) But when I saw him, I said, "What's happening, Eugene?" He looked at me like he was surprised and he said, "Would you mind repeating that?" I said it again, "What's up, Eugene?" Then he said, "You know, you're the first guy here who remembered my name." Then he started laughing and telling me what happened to him that day. We both got into a good mood and before you know it we were talking about going to a party together. But the funny thing was, he kept calling *me* Angel, and my name is Jesus!

Eugene liked Jesus because Jesus made him feel important by remembering his name when no one else did. His joy made him start confiding in Jesus about what happened that day. The two of them became friends primarily because Jesus remembered Eugene's name.

Another student, Robert, also got some interesting results. Robert had been having trouble getting dates because he was a bit overweight. But instead of sitting in class feeling sorry for himself, he decided to make something happen. He planned to memorize a classmate's name in order to get a date with her. It worked.

I met a girl with a really strange name. I had noticed how pretty she was and I heard the teacher call on her. I had to listen really carefully, a few times, before I got the full name. It turned out to be Altagracia. I wrote it down and memorized it. The next day I noticed that she was walking ahead of me as I was on my way to school. I called out to her, "Altagracia, wait up." She turned around and said, "How did you know my name?" "Oh, a pretty girl like you?" I said. "How could anyone forget your name? You're in my math class. Remember?" She said, "You know, you're the only one who has remembered my name. Everyone either forgets it or messes it up." We walked to school together and I asked her to go to see a movie with me. She accepted. All because I remembered her name.

It is possible that Altagracia may have passed up a date with young men who were even better-looking than Robert but who were not as sensitive, not interested enough or intelligent enough to realize that people like to be remembered by their names. By making Altagracia feel special, Robert got the date.

Kam Ting is usually the "shy" type, but he decided to try to see what would happen if he made a conscious effort to remember someone's name. The end result was that he not only made someone very happy, but he got himself a new friend. Here's how it happened.

I was in my gym class, running around when I saw this guy standing near the wall. I notice him every day. He stays by himself. When I finished running I went over and asked him why he wasn't running. He said he didn't feel like it. I said, "I know what you mean. What's your name?" He told me his name was David. The next day while I was running around, I saw him there by the same wall, and I called out real loud, "Hi, David." Do you know that he actually came out from that wall and started running alongside of me? We started talking together, and he was smiling and laughing with me by the end of class. I asked him if he wanted to go to the school basketball game with me. He said yes.

You can see that by remembering David's name, Kam Ting not only got David out of his "shell" but was able to get out of his own "shell" too.

Remembering people's names can do amazing things in the adult world. For example, adults will respect you more if you remember their names. Brenda had this experience.

My mother introduced a friend who works with her. The friend's name is Mrs. Taylor. Remembering what we learned about how people hate to have their names forgotten, I made an immediate plan to remember her name. I said to myself, "Her clothes look like they were custom-made by a tailor." It worked. The next time I saw my mother's friend I said, "Hello, Mrs. Taylor" with confidence, and I was sure I got it right. You could tell by the look on her face that she was happy I remembered her name, and she started talking to me. The next day, my mother told me that Mrs. Taylor said that I was a nice girl.

What made Mrs. Taylor decide that Brenda was a "nice girl"? Just the simple fact that Brenda remembered her name. People like to feel important. If you let them know that you agree with them (by remembering their names) they will like you. They will not look for further proof that you are a good person.

You have your work cut out for you. From now on, you should make it your business to concentrate on remembering people's names. Look at it as a challenge. What's the secret of doing this?

Start in the morning. On the way to school you are introduced to a friend of a friend. Repeat the name. Jot it down as soon as you get the chance. Remember it. The next day, you will feel proud when you call that person by name.

In school, pick an interesting person and call him or her by name. Begin a new relationship.

At work, learn the names of your bosses quickly. Learn the names of your co-workers and see how it affects their opinion of you.

At a party, study the names of the people to whom you're introduced. Return a few minutes later and call them by name, making a comment about something. They'll pay special attention to you because you remembered them.

After work, at home, learn the names of your family's friends. When they call on the phone, call them by name. You'll see how you rise in their esteem. They'll think you are intelligent and wonderful. The results are almost guaranteed.

Here are some charts that will help you to use the information discussed in this chapter. By doing the exercises, you will apply the things you learned in the chapter to your own life-situation, and you will see your life begin to change for the better.

_____

Record your experiences.

Remembering people's names

Where I Met the Person	*Name*	*Results*
Example: In School.	My Cherot.	He said I was intelligent.
1.		
2.		
3.		
4.		
5.		
6.		
7.		
8.		
9.		
10.		

8

Let's Just Be Happy

Teachers get grouchy sometimes. One day I was really in a bad mood. I was picking on everyone for the most minor offenses. Finally I yelled at a student who had not opened his book. I was about to threaten to lower his grade when suddenly I stopped, disarmed by the big, beautiful smile on his face. He smiled at me and kept smiling, and looking at my tense, somber face, he said, "Let's just be happy."

I had no choice but to break out into a smile too. Soon the whole class was smiling and laughing. Yes. Let's just be happy. Why do we turn minor problems into major tragedies? We're all guilty of this. The saying, A smile can melt the hardest heart has been around for a long time for a good reason. It's true. The power of a smile is amazing.

A smile radiates sunshine. It warms the atmosphere. It's like being on the beach under a cloud-filled sky, when the sun breaks through and changes everything. Suddenly it's warm and friendly. You want to stay there forever, while a few minutes before you were thinking of leaving.

A sincere smile tells you that a person likes you and accepts you. It gives you the feeling that everything is going to be fine. It gives you the courage to let down your guard toward the person smiling at you. When you smile at someone, it allows the person the chance, in turn, to let down his or her guard toward you.

Think of yourself. Do you smile a lot? Do you often break into a big, beautiful smile, or are you morose and sullen? I thought it would be difficult for young people to go around smiling at people. I hated to give that assignment because I was afraid they'd think it was foolish. But to my surprise, they didn't. They found it easy. They went out and smiled at everyone and the results were amazing.

How can you smile at someone you don't know? Try this. Think of the person you're going to smile at and say to yourself, "I want to tell you that I like you with this smile. I want to say that I'm happy to see you and I want you to know it."

It's easy to smile. Imagine yourself giving the person a gift, something warm and delightful. Then just do it—smile.

Smiling helps you to meet people. It can help you to communicate with older people too. Adults don't expect teenagers to give them a bright, sunny smile. When it comes, they can't resist it. Smiling also makes people want to help you. It also helps you to make permanent friends. Here's what happened when some teenagers tried smiling.

Maria smiled and got the attention of a young man whom she had been interested in for a long time. He worked in the supermarket where she does her shopping.

I used to go to this supermarket every week for my mother. All the time, I would notice this good-looking guy at the meat counter. So I thought about what you said about the way people have to talk to you if you smile, and I said to myself, *Why not give it a try?* So I went over to the meat counter and I waited for him to come out. Then I looked right in his face and smiled at him. He said, "May I help you?" Then he started asking me if I do the family shopping, where I hang out, and what school I go to. Before you know it he asked me if I was busy Friday night. I was so excited about this, I got all tongue-tied. Anyway, I gave him my phone number and we went out Friday night.

Rodney smiled at a woman he had often seen before and ended up feeling really good about himself by the time he got through.

I smiled at this lady on the elevator. She smiled back and asked about my high school ring. Before you know it I was telling her all about myself. We walked out of the building together and she told me that I reminded her of her son. She told me that I was one of the nicest young men in the building and that she had always admired the way I carried myself. I couldn't believe it, but when I left her I felt so happy I thought I would fly away. I had seen this woman a hundred times before, but never really bothered to make eye contact with her. Just because I looked at her and smiled we got to know each other and we both went away feeling happy.

James smiled at a bus driver and was allowed to get on the bus without the right amount of money.

I smiled at the bus driver as I was getting on the bus, and said, "Good morning." I suddenly realized that I didn't have enough money. I was a dime short, so after searching and searching for a dime, I started to get off. But the bus driver stopped me and called out,

"Get back on the bus." I told him that I didn't have the dime. He said, "That's all right." So I didn't protest. I got on. I said, "Thank you for letting me ride." He said, "No problem. I like polite people." When it was time to get off he said, "Have a good day, son." I said, "You too." We were both smiling.

Why did the bus driver let him ride? Because James brought positive attention to himself by smiling. James cheered up the driver with the energy of his smile, and the driver, not wanting to lose James's sunny presence, was more than willing to pay the dime himself. When you think of all the gloomy, dull faces on the buses and trains, it shouldn't surprise you that the driver would want to keep a happy person around.

Rosalyn smiled at a girl who she thought was stuck-up, and surprised herself by making a new friend.

As I walked to class each day, I would see this girl. She didn't talk to me and would pass by and not even look at me. This happened every time I saw her. So one day I saw her and I smiled at her as I passed her by. She smiled back. After that she would say hello every time I would go by. Then she stopped to talk to me. She said her name was Marie. Now we talk in the hall before class. I used to think she was stuck-up, but now I realize she was really just waiting to be friendly. The only reason I got to know her was because I smiled at her.

What's the point? When you smile, you put love in the air. You have the power to change your life, to make anything happen. By smiling you can make people notice you, talk to you, and become involved with you. You have this wonderful power. Why not use it? You make others happy and you can make yourself happy too.

Here are some charts that will help you to use the information discussed in this chapter. By doing the exercises, you will apply the things you learned in the chapter to your own life-situation, and you will see your life begin to change for the better.

———————

Make a record of your smiling experiences.

Place	Person	Results
Example: Lunchroom.	The girl at the next table.	We are now good friends.
1.		
2.		
3.		
4.		
5.		
6.		
7.		
8.		
9.		
10.		

9

Where'd You Get That Jacket?

When you decide that you like someone, what makes you come to that conclusion? If you think about it, it's probably because you get the feeling that that person likes you. The reverse is also true. If you meet someone and you think that he or she is "giving you dirty looks," you probably say to yourself, "I don't like that person." You say this because you interpret his or her behavior toward you as being negative.

How, then, can you let someone know that you like him or her? It's really very easy. All you have to do is study that person and say to yourself, "What do I really like about that person?" Look the person over carefully. Can you say something positive about his or her hair, eyes, teeth, body, clothing, way of talking, walking, or smiling? Can you compliment something he or she does well, like dancing, playing a sport, or telling jokes? If you think hard enough there is always something positive you can say about someone. In fact there are many things you can say. You'll probably have to be selective.

The easiest way to remove the barriers between yourself and other people, to "break the ice," is to compliment them. If you compliment people, they will immediately become receptive toward you, and look upon you as a potential friend rather than an enemy.

When you think about it, complimenting someone is really a beautiful thing to do. Wouldn't you like someone to say something positive about you? Well, in keeping with the philosophy of this book, treat other people the way you wish to be treated. Compliment them. You may be surprised to find that they want to give you compliments too—and perhaps something more. When you give from your heart, you usually receive. It seems to be an unwritten law of nature.

Eva's aunt changed her mind about taking her to Long Island when Eva complimented her home. Here's what happened.

My aunt was going to Long Island with my cousin and I really wanted to go, but my aunt didn't offer to take me. I was just sitting around the house and they were getting ready to leave. Suddenly, I thought about not just sitting there but thinking about something positive I could say to cheer my aunt up. I looked around the house and started to think about all the beautiful furniture she had. I complimented her on her fine apartment and I really meant it. I was thinking how I would like an apartment like that someday. My aunt started telling me about her new lamps, and how she had just painted the apartment. She started telling me all about the new furniture she was buying for the apartment. Then I asked her a lot of questions about decorating. As I was leaving she said, "We're going to Long Island today, would you like to go with us?" Of course, I said yes.

Because Eva complimented her aunt, her aunt opened up to her and began to communicate with her. This broke the barrier and before you know it she wanted to have Eva around and invited her to "join the party."

When Elmer complimented his friend about a jacket he was surprised to find out how willing his friend was to talk about himself.

Yesterday my friend wore this jacket that he had worn many times before. I always liked it but had never said anything. So I said, "Man, that jacket looks cool." He said, "What do you mean, I've had this jacket for a long time." I said, "I know. I've been meaning to tell you about it." Then he started telling me about the different clothes he had and that he was thinking of buying different jackets to match all his pants. Then he said how he was going to make the jacket look better. He said he was going to put a *Rocky* patch on the back. I said that would look good. Then I had to go, so I said, "I'll see you around," and I left before anything else came up. It's funny, I thought, I don't talk much, but I notice when you start complimenting someone on something, they cheer up and start telling you other things about themselves

Elmer learned how to get people involved in a conversation and found out new things about his friend.

Eddie, who has little confidence in himself in the area of ceramics, had this experience.

I walked into the ceramics class one day and the teacher took me to the basement and made me take some clay out of a tank. It was really messy. I went back upstairs and started working with the clay. I needed help but the teacher left us alone to work. I noticed this girl a few feet away was working really well with the clay. She was almost finished with her project and I thought to myself, "I wish I had her talent." I went over to the girl and said, "You know, your project is beautiful. Have you ever done this before?" She said, "No, but I work hard on it." I said, "I can see that." I kept on admiring the project. Then she picked up my ball of clay and started molding it. I said, "What are you doing?" She said, "I'll bet yours will be looking like this in no time, with a little help from me." She got me started, and before you know it I really made a beautiful vase.

Eddie started out by being frustrated with his own seeming lack of talent. He gave an honest compliment to a classmate and ended up getting help with his project.

Complimenting someone also makes it difficult for them to be severe with you. Joe was cutting class one day and was caught wandering the halls. Here's what happened to him.

The other day I was walking through the halls. I had cut out of my class early. Suddenly the assistant principal appeared. He was wearing this suit which was quite elaborate. He asked me what I was doing out of class. Before he could say another word, I told him that I liked his suit and asked him where he got it. He told me he had it made by his own private tailor. I told him that I had noticed his style in clothing. In the meantime, the bell had rung and he forgot all about asking to see my program card. He ended up saying, "Have a good day son, and go to your next class." It's funny, because I expected to get in trouble, but I did like his suit so I figured I might as well tell him so. To my amazement, I walked away free.

Joe expected to get into trouble (and perhaps he should have) but he didn't. People are so hungry for honest compliments that when they receive them they are willing to forget the rules for a moment, and just fully enjoy what is coming their way.

Sam had forgotten to do his homework in his American Studies class and the teacher was annoyed. After apologizing for not doing his homework, Sam reports:

I told him the truth, that his class is the only one I have never cut. I also said that I noticed he really cared for his students. He was quiet for a while and then said, "I'm very flattered. You know you are one of my best students." He kept on saying good things about me.

Sam's sincere compliment not only calmed the teacher's anger but got him a compliment in return.

When you compliment people, they seem to get so excited they don't know what to say first. The reason for this is that so few people take the time to say what they are thinking about someone. You often look at someone and say to yourself, "I really like her hairstyle." But how often do you tell the person? People can go around week after week looking wonderful, but they won't know it—not until *you* tell them.

Willie's friend Mike became so happy when Willie complimented his hair that he was no longer ashamed of the bald spot on his head.

I was walking down the street and I met my friend Mike. He's bald on the top of his head and has long hair on the sides. When I saw him I noticed he had gotten a haircut, so I said, "Mike, your hair looks nice and neat." He said, "Thank you." Then I asked him where he got it cut. He said, "I did it myself." I said, "Wow, you did a great job." He looked very proud and moved around a little. I said, "You should keep it like that all the time. It makes you look younger." Then he started telling me all about what he does to keep his hair looking good. I forgot to mention that he had a hat on when I saw him. After the compliment he took the hat off and put it in his pocket.

Eddie's compliment worked to make Mike proud of himself, proud enough to not want to hide the bald spot on the top of his head.

When you compliment someone about a skill that they have, you encourage them to become even better. Tony complimented his brother's skill at basketball and here's what happened.

I complimented my older brother and told him that he was a great basketball player. You should have heard him talk. He told me he never lost a game and that he had been given an offer to play for the Boston

Celtics. After that he said he was going down to practice, and asked if I wanted to join him.

I'm sure Tony's brother played better than ever that day.
Jeanie had a similar experience with her mother.

On Friday night my mother and I were doing exercises
together to keep in shape. When we finished I told
her that she was losing weight and looked great. After
I told her how good she looked, she started doing
some more exercises. She was smiling and talking
about how she could do anything she wanted if she
put her mind to it.

Jeanie's compliment spurred her mother on to do even more.
Did you know that a compliment at the right time can make
the difference between giving up or going on? Just think of
the power you have just by saying a few words.

Here are some charts that will help you to use the information discussed in this chapter. By doing the exercises, you will apply the things you learned in the chapter to your own life-situation, and you will see your life begin to change for the better.

———————

Make a list of your "complimenting" experiences.

Name	Compliment	Results
Example: Mr. Jones, Principal.	His beautiful tie.	Smiled and said that I was observant.
1.		
2.		
3.		
4.		
5.		
6.		
7.		
8.		
9.		
10.		

10

You Can't Listen with Your Mouth Open

We all love to talk about ourselves. "I'm going to do this." "I did that." "Did I ever tell you about the time I . . ."

Talking about yourself is natural. It's a sign of vitality. It means you are excited about what's going on in your life. How do you feel about people who are interested in listening to you talk about yourself? You probably can't wait to see them so that you can tell them the latest thing going on in your life.

Well, think about it for a moment. How will people feel about you if you show a genuine interest in what they have to say? Sometimes it isn't easy. We're so concerned with our own lives that we're just waiting for the other guy to shut up so we can start talking about ourselves. Half the time we're not really listening to what someone else has to say. But if you talk only about yourself, people will avoid you.

If you want to be that rare person who is loved and respected, stop for a moment and really listen to what people are saying. Ask them questions about themselves. Before you know it, people will tell you what they're excited about, what they dream of, what they've accomplished, and what bothers them.

The end result of this kind of listening will be that you're in demand. People will begin to look for you when something exciting happens to them. You'll be the first one they want to talk to.

Why do people have the need to talk about themselves anyway? Once again, think about yourself. How do you feel when you're alone in the house all day with no one to talk to? It can be depressing. Before you know it, you call someone on the telephone, just to talk. Talking to people makes you feel alive.

It also gives you reinforcement. If you have a wonderful idea, the first thing you want to do is talk about it with someone who is receptive, who can say, "Hey, that sounds good." This reinforcement spurs you on to follow through with the idea. It gives you energy.

Talking to people also helps you to understand yourself better. After talking for a while you begin to see the solution to your own problem. Sometimes all you need is a good listener.

People will really appreciate you if you are a good listener. But more than that, and here's the irony, people will believe that you're intelligent, just because you listen to them. They'll think you are mature and interesting and will talk about you when you're not around. "He's some conversationalist," or "She's got a good head on her shoulders." And whether you truly are what they say, in a sense, they're right. You have to be intelligent to realize the importance of listening.

The next time you're with some people, and you catch yourself doing a lot of talking about yourself, stop. Ask yourself the question, "How can I get the other person to begin talking about himself or herself?" But remember, you have to be genuinely interested in the person and not merely going through the motions.

Here are some stories that may help you to get some ideas. A group of high school students had the following experiences.

Wilfred caught himself doing too much talking. When he stopped, this is what happened.

I'm an artist. My hobby is drawing and painting. Saturday, a friend's cousin came to spend the night over at his house. He's also an artist. My friend brought him over to meet me, so I let them in and led them to my room where most of my pictures are hung on the wall. He saw the pictures and complimented me on them. Then I started talking about my work, my talent, my goals, etc. Suddenly I realized that I was talking about myself too much. I immediately started asking him a lot of questions about his work. Sure enough, his face lit up and he started talking and talking. This lasted for at least forty-five minutes. After that he asked if we could get together that evening to talk some more about art. I said yes.

The young man was interested in getting together with Wilfred because Wilfred was interested in him. Think of what would have happened if Wilfred hadn't caught himself, but continued to go on and on about himself. The young man would probably have been waiting for an opportunity to escape.

People want to be around you when you let them talk about themselves. It happened with Wilfred, and it happened with Simone. But in Simone's case, it was with a previously indifferent boyfriend.

I had been dating this guy Ronnie, and whenever I was with him I talked about myself. But then I learned about getting people to talk about themselves. Since I knew he loved sports, I started asking him lots of questions about basketball. He told me how many exercises he does, how many trophies he had won, and lots of other things. Then he told me all about his swimming team. He wouldn't let me get a word in edgewise! Now he calls me all the time.

Another thing that happens when you let people talk about themselves is that they become generous with you. You have given them a gift by letting them express themselves, and they feel so happy that they automatically want to give you something in return. Here's what happened to Mark.

On Sunday my family had a portrait photo taken. We couldn't have individual pictures taken, because my father couldn't afford it. While the photographer was working I started to wonder how he got into photography. After the picture was taken, I asked him how he got started. He told me all about how he had loved cameras when he was a kid. He went on and on, telling me about all of his equipment and how it worked. By the time he was through, not only did he take my

picture alone, but he told me that I was very photo-
genic. He then volunteered to take a picture of me
and my girl friend too.

Susan got to know her mother better by listening.

My mother and I were watching a TV show on about
the fifties. I asked her what it was like in those days.
She told me that she used to wear dungarees and a
garrison belt and sweaters backwards with a necker-
chief. She said she hung out with a bunch of people
who were in a gang and that she was the leader of the
girls' division. She told me about all her boyfriends
and that there weren't so many drugs then and much
less crime. She got really happy talking about how
she used to be when she was a teenager. When I went
to bed that night, I started thinking about my mother,
how she was once a teenager like me. I started to cry
because I never really thought about it before, and I
loved her more.

Whether people give you something or not, listening to
people gives you a new way of looking at things. It's an
education that cannot be gained from books. In Susan's case
it brought her closer to her mother in a most beautiful way.

Here are some charts that will help you to use the information discussed in this chapter. By doing the exercises, you will apply the things you learned in the chapter to your own life-situation, and you will see your life begin to change for the better.

Make a list of your listening experiences.

Person	Topic of Conversation	Results
Example: My friend.	His weight training.	Asked me to go with him to the gym and I did. Now I train too.

1.

2.

3.

4.

5.

6.

7.

8.

9.

10.

11

So You Had a Fight with Your Mother

Now let's take listening a step further. Let's add caring. What this amounts to is compassion: putting yourself in the place of someone else with a serious problem and really showing concern. Make believe it was you with that problem.

Let's say you had a fight with your mother. You go to school very upset and run into a friend. "What's wrong?" the friend says. "Oh, I had this big fight with my mother just before leaving for school. I'm so mad that I feel like cutting class." Your friend says, "Tell me what started it." As you talk, your friend says, "I know what you mean," "She did that?" "Wow, I can't believe it," "You must have been furious," etc. etc. Your friend is showing you that he or she can imagine just how you feel. In effect, your friend is being compassionate.

Everyone has problems. People have broken up with boyfriends and girl friends. People lose their wallets. They fail tests. They get in trouble at home. They get fired from jobs. They get into fights. They need someone who is willing to sympathize with them, someone who cares.

If you learn how to be a compassionate listener to people with problems, you'll be a friend of that person for life. It's really easy to imagine. Just think of how you feel about someone who listens sympathetically to you. It could be a friend, a teacher, or a parent. You love that person. You really appreciate them.

Now think about this. When was the last time someone started telling you about a problem? Did you just try to shut them up as quickly as possible so you could get on with your own business?

Say, for example, someone loses their bus pass. They are very upset and tell you about it. You say, "That's a shame," and walk away. Would you like someone to do that to you? Wouldn't you feel better if they listened to the whole story of how you lost it, and then maybe offered to help you get another one?

Why should you bother to listen to people's problems? Because you have a heart, that's why. In order to be fully human, you have to give in to that big beautiful heart of yours, to become the loving person that you really are inside. By putting yourself in the place of someone else, by feeling their pain for a moment, you become a special person.

When you empathize with someone, you grow. Another strange thing happens, though. You find that when you have problems, people empathize with you. It seems to have a boomerang effect.

Still another strange thing happens when you empathize. You have a special, warm feeling inside. Time and again, students have reported to me that when they help someone by listening to their problems, they not only leave the person feeling much better, but they also feel as if they were walking on air.

Naturally, you can only listen to so many problems. After all, you are not a psychiatrist. But at least be aware of opportunities to show compassion. I asked a group of high school students whether or not they listen to people's problems. Most of them admitted that they try to get the person off their back as soon as possible, and that they felt slightly guilty about it.

If this is true for you, don't feel bad. You are not alone. It's human nature to want to avoid things that are unpleasant. But you can break that pattern. By showing concern you can turn the unpleasant into the pleasant. Don't run away from a challenge, face it head-on. Think of it as a chance to make something happen. The next time someone has a problem and you catch yourself making an excuse to get away, stop and really listen. Imagine yourself in the same situation. See what happens.

Here's what happened to some high school students who decided to reverse their previous behavior. Freddy got involved with his teacher's problems.

Last week during class, I noticed that my teacher was snapping at everyone. I said to him, "I don't know how you put up with all of us. We make so much noise, we come late, and then we all attack you at once. If I were you, I'd probably go crazy." "Oh, I get along," he said. "It's just that I had a problem with my car this morning. It overheated on the way to school and I got to work late. I have to buy a new car soon. That car has been giving me nothing but trouble lately." We talked about cars for a while. By the time the bell rang he was happy and smiling. He wished me a good day, and he got up and started walking like he didn't have a care in the world. I left feeling really happy too. I was grinning from ear to ear.

Why did the teacher walk away so happy? Because Freddy gave him the opportunity to tell someone about the car overheating. As a result the teacher thinks well of him. He even wished him a good day. What he was really saying is, "I hope some good comes to you. Thank you for cheering me up."

Monique sympathized with the clerk in the supermarket and he ended up asking her for a date.

Yesterday while walking into the supermarket, I noticed this good-looking guy at the register. I did my shopping and waited on line. There was a lady in front of me who was arguing with him. He kept his cool but I could see she was really getting to him. Later, when she left, I said, "Gee, it must be hard working around people all day." "You're not kidding," he said. "Some of them are really nasty." I asked him what happened with the lady who had just left, and he told me how she was blaming him for something that was spoiled, even though he tried to explain that she should tell the store manager. "That's ridiculous," I said. "You shouldn't have to put up with such abuse." Then he seemed much happier. "It's a job," he said, "and I need the money." Then he said he had a break coming up, and asked me if I would like to join him for lunch. I said okay, and after lunch we ended up making a date for Friday night.

Sherry sympathized with a girl and prevented her from running away from home.

I was talking to this girl I had just met about her relationship with her mother. She said she wanted to run away from home because of the way her mother treated her. I kept saying, "I understand how you feel. My mother sometimes does that too. I know how it can get to you." After we finished talking, she said, "Sherry, you know, you're really a nice person." She told me she was going to call me the next day after school. She called me and she said she decided it wasn't so bad at home after all, especially when you have friends you can talk to. I felt really good. I didn't even know how much I had helped her until she told me she wasn't thinking about running away from home anymore.

When you think of how much good you can do by just being sympathetic, I'm sure you'll want to try it. A comforting word at the right moment might even prevent someone from committing suicide. You never know. You just never know when the person with a problem is that desperate.

Recently a young girl in our school jumped out of a fifth-floor window in her building and plunged to her death. It turned out that she was pregnant and felt that she had no one to turn to. My class discussed it and many of the students said, "I wish I could have talked to her." Some of the students admitted that they might have been too busy or too caught up with their own problems to listen to her. Others claimed that they would have been able to help her.

What would you have done? Are you the type of person who stops and listens, or do you brush people off? Why not make a special effort to try to listen to people's problems. Perhaps your experiences will be even more dramatic than the ones in this book.

Here are some charts that will help you to use the information discussed in this chapter. By doing the exercises, you will apply the things you learned in the chapter to your own life-situation, and you will see your life begin to change for the better.

Make a list of your listening experiences concerning people's problems.

Person	Problem	Results
Example: A girl in English.	She lost her wallet.	We are now friends.

1.

2.

3.

4.

5.

6.

7.

8.

9.

10.

12

Luck Is in the Air!

Kevin won the lottery. Regina was picked to be prom queen. Allan found a fifty-dollar bill. What luck!

"Some people have all the luck." Ever hear someone say that, with resentment in his or her voice? Do you ever feel as if other people seem to get all the breaks in life?

This is a chapter on success, whether it is a "lucky break" or a combination of hard work and a little luck.

Why is it that we sometimes feel threatened when someone else does well? It seems as if there's an illogical superstition that there is just so much luck available, and if other people get lucky, it means the rest of us will be left out. But this notion is ridiculous. *Luck is in the air.* Bring it down upon yourself by celebrating other people's luck. Your time will come.

In the meantime, why not get excited about someone else's good fortune or achievements? Why not celebrate with them as if it were you who had the windfall? After all, think of how you feel when something fantastic happens to you. You just can't wait to tell your friends. But what if they were totally indifferent to the great news? You'd feel terrible, wouldn't you? So why not make believe it's you and get into it. You'll surprise yourself by actually feeling their joy once you start. Suppose a good friend tells you that he made the football team. You could say, "Oh, that's nice," and walk away. Or, you could say, "Wow. I can't believe it. How did you do it? We have to celebrate."

How will your friend feel about you if you celebrate his victory? How will he react when you tell him about a wonderful event in your life? Naturally, he will be inclined to celebrate with you. The biblical adage "Give and it shall be given unto you" seems to apply here.

Why don't we automatically get excited about other people's good news? The answer is quite simple. We're concerned about ourselves. We get so caught up in our own lives that we forget others exist.

How much will you benefit by being generous with your good wishes? More than you can imagine. First of all, the person will appreciate your generosity of spirit and you will probably gain a deeper friendship. You may even find, to your surprise, that they will share with you some of their good fortune. Finally, you will make that person so happy that the happiness will flow onto you.

I asked some high school students to try it and they said it was the easiest thing I had asked them to do. It seems as if someone is always celebrating something. Do you agree?

When Maria congratulated her boyfriend for making a good speech he began to appreciate her more.

My boyfriend came to pick me up Tuesday and he was very excited because he had just made a speech. He told me he was glad everyone liked the speech and that he was very nervous before he gave it. I remembered what you said about congratulating people, and I said in a very happy voice, "Congratulations. You were great. I'm really proud of you." He got so happy he started kissing me and telling me that he wants me to be a big part of his life. Then he asked me if I wanted to go out and celebrate with him. He had a smile on his face that you wouldn't believe, and it made me feel fantastic.

Another student congratulated his friend when he got a new job and deepened his friendship as a result.

My friend Jim, who had been unemployed for a while, got a job the other day. At first, I didn't care about it. Then I remembered about getting excited with people about their good fortune, so I said, "Jim, congratulations. That's wonderful news. Tell me all about the job." Then we talked about the job for a while. After the conversation Jim turned to me and said, "You're a real friend." The funny thing was that at first I didn't even want to congratulate him, but I forced myself. I'm really glad I did because it made him so happy, and it made me see how important I can be as a friend.

People need you more than you can imagine. When you meet people's needs, your own needs are met.

Stanley wished his brother well on a simple thing like his birthday and changed the whole environment that day.

Last Monday was my brother's birthday. When he got up that morning he was waiting for someone to say happy birthday, but everybody forgot. So I remembered, and I said, "Happy Birthday, Greg. How does it feel to be fourteen years old?" He smiled broadly and said, "Great." Then he said, "Thanks for remembering my birthday." Then he started strutting around the house singing. *I* felt good because I had made *him* feel good, and when I left for school that morning I wasn't as grouchy as usual.

Because Stanley took the time to make his brother happy, he got the benefit of his brother's joy. He fought the temptation to say "The hell with him. What about me? It sounds stupid anyway, saying, 'Happy Birthday, how does it feel?'" He decided to go out of his way and say something nice. His words were worth more than money. They gave joy, something money can't buy.

You would be surprised what might happen when you join people in celebrating their good luck. Here's what happened to Sandra.

My aunt won five hundred dollars in a lottery. The first thing my sister said to her was, "Hey, why don't you give me some money." I just said, "Congratulations. You deserve it. You could do a lot with that money." A few days later my aunt came over to see my mother. She had a package with her. She gave it to me and said, "Here, I bought you a little surprise." It was a gold chain I'd been wanting for a long time. I was really surprised.

The worst thing in the world you can say to someone who has just won money is, "Give me some." What you're really saying is, "Who cares about you? I'm looking out for my-self." If you give someone this message, it will make the person feel bad. Notice that Sandra, and not her sister, got the reward.

Of course, Sandra had no idea that her aunt would bring her a present; she merely wanted her aunt to enjoy her good luck and she was genuinely expressing her happiness. Iron-ically, by being selfish and asking for money, Sandra's sister got nothing. Because Sandra treated her aunt the way she wished to be treated, she got the surprise.

Often, when you congratulate someone they will want to honor you. Here's what happened to Jason.

Once my little cousin joined a Junior League baseball team. He was really happy, but no one even con-gratulated him. I was the only one to say, "You're amazing, Peter. I'm proud of you, congratulations." Now he says that every time he plays he thinks about me.

Sometimes when you congratulate someone, they'll want to make you a part of the "lucky event." Here's what hap-pened to Joanne.

When my aunt found out that she was pregnant, she became so happy that she came running over to tell my mother. But my mother said, "Don't you have enough headaches with the two you already have?" That made my aunt feel really bad. Then I came in and congratulated her and said, "That's wonderful. What are you hoping for this time?" That cheered her right up again and she offered to make me the baby's godmother.

When people have something to celebrate, they don't need anyone bringing out the negative part of it. What they do need is for you to help them celebrate. Who did the aunt want her baby's godmother to be, the negative commentator or the congratulator?

Let's face the facts. There are "down" people and "up" people in life. Down people (let's call them negative) always have some point to make about what is wrong with a situation. Up people (let's call them positive) always seem to emphasize the positive side and to be ready to celebrate a victory.

Winners and losers. You can pick them out. The winner says, "Congratulations on your engagement. You're really lucky." The loser says, "But you're so young, it will end up in a divorce." The winner says, "I'm glad you got the job." The loser says, "Man, how can you work for such a low salary?" The winner says, "I'm glad you placed second in the swimming competition." The loser says, "Too bad you couldn't make first place."

Get the picture? The winner says, "I'm glad something good happened to you." The loser says, "I'm jealous of you. I hope you have bad luck."

Of course, no one says those things directly, but that is what's really behind their attitude.

Be generous. Everyone has the ability to be an "up" person. All it takes is practice. Challenge yourself to find opportunities to celebrate other people's good fortune. Your day will come, and when it does, I guarantee you will have other people to celebrate with you.

Here are some charts that will help you to use the information discussed in this chapter. By doing the exercises, you will apply the things you learned in the chapter to your own life-situation, and you will see your life begin to change for the better.

———————

Make a list of things you congratulated people for. Keep a going record.

Person	Event	Results
Example: My mother.	She got a promotion at her job.	She hugged me and said, "now we are in the money."

1.

2.

3.

4.

5.

6.

7.

8.

9.

10.

13

You're Not Like All Those Other...

When dealing with people, what you expect is usually what you will get. Take the case of the typical class clown. Everyone expects Jared to make some joke to disrupt the class, and so Jared, living up to his reputation, doesn't disappoint people. He disrupts the class with a joke. But if someone used psychology, and gave Jared a different reputation to live up to, things might be different. Say, for example, someone said that Jared really had a serious side to him, and was capable of some pretty deep ideas. Before you know it, Jared would be asking serious questions in class, living up to his reputation as the class philosopher.

When dealing with people, if you want to bring out the best in them, why not expect the best from them? The psychology is really quite simple. Most people want to be thought of as having fine qualities. When you let someone know that you believe he has this quality, even if he has not yet demonstrated it, he will quickly make every effort to bring out the quality, to prove that your high opinion of him is right.

In dealing with people, it's important to understand what it takes to bring out their best qualities. If you want to be able to control situations that might otherwise get out of hand, to be able to help people become their most admirable selves, to change a person's behavior toward you from negative to positive, you should know how to give someone a fine reputation to live up to.

Why do people respond to the idea that they are more noble or more virtuous than they already are? Perhaps it's because deep down they know that they can be. Maybe they have even thought about improving their behavior. When someone comes along and already sees them as fine people, it gives them the power to take action.

Take the case of Mary, for example. Some young men were going to be fresh with her, but before she got finished with them, they were behaving as if they were perfect gentlemen. Here's what happened.

One day my friend and I were bored. We were sitting in front of the building and we noticed these guys that used to hang out with my older sister sitting across the street looking at us. They came over and asked if they could join us. We said yes, and then they asked us to go for a ride in their truck. Now, we knew these guys. One of them worked in the supermarket around the corner. But once we were in the truck, riding, I began to get scared. What were they up to?
I decided to give them a fine reputation to live up to. I said, "Man, you guys are all right. I mean, I really

had the wrong impression of you before, but you're not like all those other guys that get fresh as soon as they have some girls alone in a car." I kept adding to it and really going into it, so that they treated us beautifully. But in the meantime, I know that they were planning to get fresh, but I had praised them so much they were ashamed to try anything.

Interesting. Why were they "ashamed to try anything"? Evidently, they liked being thought of as gentlemen.

Billie gave his friend a fine reputation to live up to, and his friend cleaned up his apartment.

My friend has a nice apartment, but it's a real mess. When I went up there, I told him that he had a really nice apartment. He said thank you. When I told him that, he started cleaning up. Then I said that it was nicely decorated even though I had said to myself, "It's kind of bare." When I told him that it was nicely decorated he said, "Just a minute, I'll be right back." I had to wait fifteen minutes for him, but when he came back he had some different colored lights to put around the apartment.

What would have happened if Billie had said, "This place is a mess and you are a hopeless slob who doesn't know how to decorate an apartment?" More than likely, Billie's friend would have gotten very annoyed, and he probably would have continued to be sloppy and indifferent.

Anyone can just blurt out what they're thinking, but it takes an intelligent person to stop and think before speaking. It pays to ask yourself, "What will his or her reaction be to what I say?" And, "How can I use psychology in order to help this person?"

Here's what happened to Reggie.

There was a guy on my running team who used to wear the same pair of shorts for a month. I mean they were supposed to be white, but they were gray from dirt and he smelled awful. But he did have a pretty girl friend. One day the team was teasing him. He was mad and getting ready to defend himself. I stole everyone's attention by saying, "Man, he can't be too dirty because he's got that girl. I know she wouldn't like dirty, smelly people." He chimed in, "Yeah man, I take a bath every night." We all knew he was lying, because the dude really did stink. Everyone just laughed and left it alone. In a few days he was wearing clean shorts, and he even lost that awful smell.

By pointing out a positive aspect of the young man's life (that he did have a pretty girl friend), Reggie helped the young man to see that he had something going for him. This motivated him to want to care about his appearance and hygiene. Notice that he bragged about taking a bath every night. In reality, what he was saying was, "I should take a bath every night." Now that people were giving him respect, he could actually do what he knew he should do. He did it and there was a change in his appearance, all because someone gave him a fine reputation to live up to.

By giving a person a positive image to live up to, you could make a loser into a winner. Here's what happened to Sharon.

I have always played handball better than anybody on my block. I can even beat the boys. One day I asked this boy to play and he said, "Okay, I'll play you, but I know you're going to beat me." I decided to give him a reputation to live up to. I said, "Oh, no. I'm scared of you, you're a strong player. I've seen you play." Then he said, "Okay." In the meantime, I said to myself, "I'll probably beat the pants off him." But once the game started, this guy began killing me. The score was six to two. No matter how hard I tried, he kept advancing points. Before you know it, he won, nine to three. Maybe he would have won anyway, but I doubt it. Then he went around telling everybody that he beat me. Just because I gave him a fine reputation to live up to, he actually did beat me. I couldn't believe it.

Does your mother seem to yell at you more than you'd like? Does your boyfriend have the bad habit of always being late? Does your girl friend forget to call when she says she will? Is your little brother grouchy or sloppy? Is your teacher impatient? Why not give these people a fine reputation to live up to? If you do you will see a definite change in their behavior.

People will tend to rise to the compliment. They don't want to disappoint you. It even worked on me. One day I was in the elevator, and a teacher said, "You're always so pleasant and you always say good morning." But I was feeling grouchy that day and I was thinking about not even speaking. After that, whenever I saw him in the halls, I made sure I gave him a hearty "Good morning." Why? I had to. I wasn't going to let him think less of me. I like being thought of as pleasant. And after that, I tried to be pleasant to people more than ever.

See how it works. Dale Carnegie, in his book *How to Win Friends and Influence People*, said, "Give the dog a good name." In other words, call a dog bad and he'll bite you. Say, "Good boy, good boy," and he'll probably lick you. What's it going to be? Are you going to get licked or bitten?

Here are some charts that will help you to use the information discussed in this chapter. By doing the exercises, you will apply the things you learned in the chapter to your own life-situation, and you will see your life begin to change for the better. –

———————————

Make a list of the times you gave someone a fine reputation to live up to. Record the results.

Person	Reputation	Change in Behavior
Example: School custodian.	"You always clean so well."	The room was cleaner than ever the next day.
1.		
2.		
3.		
4.		
5.		
6.		
7.		
8.		
9.		
10.		

14

But I Get Around

Have you ever found yourself in the embarrassing situation of wanting to criticize someone without hurting his or her feelings? Say, for example, your best friend has bad breath, or someone sitting next to you in class should use deodorant. What can you do?

Well, the worst thing you could possibly do, of course, is to just blurt out the cold, hard facts. There are ways to give constructive criticism without offending the person you are trying to correct. You can call attention to the person's fault indirectly so that he or she doesn't perceive your criticism as an attack. You can also try criticizing yourself first and then gently bringing in the criticism about the person. Another way to help a person to cope with your criticism is to give that person a compliment first. This softens the blow. It helps to put the criticism into perspective.

In order to understand how to criticize the right way, let's look at an example of the *wrong* way to criticize. This is what happened to Barbara.

I was with my cousin and I always hate to see her because she's so fat. So I decided to tell her what I really thought. I said, "Man, Rosa, you're so fat. Why don't you go on a diet? Those pants don't even look right on you." She got mad and cursed me out. We kept putting each other down. Then I left. After that I apologized, but she still can't stand me.

Barbara's mistake is obvious. She called direct attention to Rosa's problem, and Rosa took it as an insult and began to defend herself. What did Barbara gain by directly exposing Rosa? Nothing. In fact she lost a friend, even though Rosa was her cousin.

Barbara had good intentions. How should she have gone about criticizing Rosa? If Barbara had been more gentle, complimenting Rosa first, Rosa might have been more inclined to go on a diet. She could have said, "Rosa, you are such a beautiful girl. But if you could lose some weight, you would be even more beautiful." Then Rosa might have said, "Yes, I really want to go on a diet." Barbara could have then suggested a good diet and a plan to stick to that diet. The next thing you know, Rosa might have been well on her way to being in perfect shape.

Barbara might also have reached Rosa by criticizing herself first. She could have said, "I'm so skinny, I have to do something about my body. My clothes just hang on me. I think I'll go to a gym and work out so I can build myself up. After all, I want to look good. Why don't we both do something to improve ourselves?" Rosa might have suggested a diet herself.

If you criticize yourself first, people do not feel threatened. You're no longer posing as a judge. They don't feel that you are saying that you are better than they are, and will be more likely to listen to what you have to say.

Another way to offer constructive criticism is to call attention to the person's problem area indirectly. Barbara could have said, "Are those new pants? What size are they?" Then she could have said, "I'll bet you could be one size less in two weeks if you wanted to be." In this instance Rosa would have had a chance to think about her problem by herself rather than be exposed by Barbara. By asking questions and thus indirectly criticizing Rosa, Barbara could have helped Rosa to see that she didn't look great in the pants, and that she needed to lose weight.

If you gain someone's trust and confidence, the person won't feel threatened by criticism because he or she will understand that you're trying to help, not to hurt or belittle. So compliment the person first, criticize yourself first, or draw attention to the problem indirectly.

These three methods of criticism will help you get your message across to a friend you want to help. If you care about your friends you can't just ignore a problem that could be corrected. You can't let your friend go around wearing clothes that are too tight when you know that everyone is talking about her. You can't let your brother continue doing things that might result in his being suspended or expelled from school.

Some people may tell you that you should mind your own business. But this *is* your business. Your friends and relatives are a part of your life and in this sense, a part of your business. To ignore a blatant fault in someone you care for is like asking yourself to walk by a crooked picture on the wall every day, and to just leave it that way. You will always be tempted to straighten it out. Sooner or later you will, so applying the analogy to criticism, you might as well know *how* to straighten it out so that it will not fall off the wall and crush your toe.

Since it is natural and sometimes necessary to criticize, wouldn't it be great if you could learn to do it so that people would not only accept the criticism, but thank you for it?

Here are examples of each of the three methods of criticism. In each case the person being critical did not lose his or her friend, and was appreciated for trying to help.

Jennifer used the method of complimenting first when she couldn't believe that her friend was wearing a pair of ugly socks to a birthday party.

I was going to a birthday party Saturday night and I went to Rosalee's house to pick her up. She was wearing a beautiful blouse, pants, and shoes. Everything matched and looked great, except for the thick sweat socks she had on. They looked terrible. She asked me how she looked. I said, "You look beautiful. I love your blouse and pants. Where did you get them?" She told me they were a gift from her mother. She was really happy. Then I said, "Rosalee, your whole outfit looks great, but those socks really don't go with it. If you would just change those socks and put on some stockings or knee-high's, you would look perfect." Would you believe it? She agreed with me and took off the socks and put on some stockings. We had a great time at the party. She thanked me a few times for tipping her off about the socks.

Jennifer was a true friend: someone who will tell you how to look your best, but will deliver the criticism with love and care. We are all really fragile, you know. If you "drop" something on us, we "break."

Diana got someone to accept her criticism by talking about her own faults first.

In my job there was this new guy, so I had to watch him and make sure everything was right. He kept on making the ice cream scoops too small. I told him to make them bigger and he seemed upset. Then, when the customers left, he looked depressed, so I said, "You should have seen me when I first started. I made a mess of the milkshakes." Then we talked about my mistakes and we both started laughing. Then I explained to him how to scoop ice cream and he accepted it, so I didn't have to get nasty with him. After a while he started to do them right. By talking about my own mistakes, he didn't think that I was trying to put myself above him.

Ronnie used the third method of criticism. He called attention to his friend's fault indirectly and helped him to improve his paddleball game.

One time I was playing paddleball, which is my favorite sport. This guy who recently moved around the block was trying to play but he kept losing, so I started talking to him. I told him that he made a few good shots but if he would only hit a little more directly it would probably be better. Then I showed him some ways to hit without telling him his way was all wrong. Then he started again and he won five games that afternoon. He thanked me and said I was all right. He was a sad person on the court before, but he left a happy guy because of me.

Evidently Ronnie was quite proud of actually causing the new guy's game to improve and making him happy. He used his energy and his intelligence to help someone rather than put him down.

There are people who go around trying to put you down. Their goal is not to give you constructive criticism but to make you feel bad. Why do they do this? Simple. They feel inferior and believe that by insulting you enough you will become even lower than they are. They foolishly believe that in this way they will be "above" you. Such people have problems with self-esteem.

But if you're not careful, you may appear to be one of those people who put others down. Even if your intentions are good, you can be misunderstood and your criticism may be rejected. That is why it's so important to use psychology when attempting to correct someone.

Here are some charts that will help you to use the information discussed in this chapter. By doing the exercises, you will apply the things you learned in the chapter to your own life-situation, and you will see your life begin to change for the better.

———————

Make a list of your criticizing experiences. Record the results.

Person	Criticism	Results
Example: My friend.	"Your makeup looks beautiful, but it hides your natural beauty. Why not try less?"	She didn't wear half as much the next day.

1.

2.

3.

4.

5.

6.

7.

8.

9.

10.

15

You're Wrong!

_____

The best way to get into a hot argument with someone is to say, *You're wrong*. Those are definitely fighting words. If this is true, why is it that we so often hear people saying them?

People simply do not think about the consequences of their words. If they did, they would plan what they say rather than just blurt things out. If you want to convince someone that you are right and he or she is wrong, wouldn't it be intelligent to find a way to cause that person to have an open mind toward you, rather than using words that will close his or her mind from the start?

What happens when you tell someone, "You're wrong"? First of all, the person thinks that you are saying, "I know more than you do, I am smarter than you." If you think about it for a moment, no one in the world likes to be told outright that you are smarter than he or she is. Even though we all know there are people around who are more intelligent than we are, we don't appreciate being told so outright. So when you tell someone, "You're wrong," the first thing the person does is think, "We'll see about that. I'll show you that I am right."

In order to see if this is true, I asked some high school students to go out and find opportunities to tell people they were wrong. Invariably the students reported that they got into trouble. Here's what happened to Wilbert.

A friend came over to my house. We were in my room looking at comic books when I told him that the Hulk never fought the X-Men. He said he was pretty sure they did. Then I said, "You're wrong. How could you be so stupid?" Then I continued to insist that the Hulk never fought the X-Men. At this point he was boiling. He called me an idiot. One thing led to another and he left. As he was walking out he met my younger brother and I heard him tell him that I was stupid. I felt bad because we were supposed to go to a movie together later, but I was too mad to call him that day.

Wilbert did the wrong thing deliberately to prove a point to himself and he almost lost a friend. How many times do you do the wrong thing just by not taking control of yourself? How many unnecessary arguments do you get into?

What should Wilbert have done if he wanted to prove his point without alienating his friend? Well, first of all, he should have been more careful about how he made his statements. For example, he could have said, "I may be wrong, but I could swear that the Hulk never fought the X-Men. Let me doublecheck and I'll bet you know what I find out. I'll be amazed if I'm wrong, but you never know." By having this attitude, Wilbert's friend wouldn't have had anything to fight about. All he could say is, "We'll see what happens when you find out." Wilbert would have calmed himself down as well. A head-on confrontation only leads to one thing: a crash and then pain.

When you tell people they're wrong, they will go to great lengths to prove that they are right. Darlene tried the assignment with an adult, and was amazed by what happened.

I was talking on the phone with this lady who knows my mother and she told me that she had just seen this private production of *Macbeth* up in Vermont, and she was telling me about how well the people spoke their lines, and she quoted this one line: "Will all great Neptune's oceans wash this blood clean from my hand?" She said that Macbeth said that, and I said, "You're wrong. Lady Macbeth said that, and that's why she kept washing her hands." Then the lady said to me, "Are you trying to tell me that I am wrong? I have been studying Shakespeare's plays for many years, and I should know. Macbeth says that in act two, scene two, pages seventy-eight to seventy-nine in the Folger Library edition of *Macbeth*." I still insisted, "No, you're wrong." With that she hung up on me. A few minutes later she called back and said she was coming over to prove that she was right. Then the doorbell rang and it was her. She was huffing and puffing like a bull and she stomped in and had the play in her hands. She shoved the book in front of my face and said, "Look here," and showed me the part. I said, "I must have confused the line with Lady Macbeth's line." She said, "You sure did." Then she calmed down and said that she didn't mean to get angry, but that she was upset that I told her that she was wrong.

If Darlene had calmly stated that she was almost sure that the line was Lady Macbeth's, but she would recheck to be sure, the lady would never have come to her house in a rage. It's all a matter of pride. Don't step on someone's ego or you'll have the devil to pay.

Disputed facts cause a lot of arguments. Both Wilbert and Darlene (in their cases, deliberately) made the mistake of saying "You're wrong," instead of saying, "Wait, let's check the facts."

There are other ways to fall into the trap of saying "You're wrong." One of the most tempting occasions is when you don't agree with someone else's opinion on a given issue. When you find yourself arguing with someone about a thing that cannot be proven, the best thing to do is to listen to the other person's opinion, to tell them that they have a good point, and then to state your own opinion. Then you can peacefully end the conversation by saying, "You have a right to your opinion and I have a right to mine. We don't have to agree on everything in order to be friends, do we?"

Simone tried this in the middle of a hot argument.

The other day my friend and I went swimming, and while we were in the locker room we had a disagreement. I said that when a guy buys you gifts, it really means he cares for you. She said it doesn't mean a thing, it just means he has money. We started arguing and yelling at each other. I was so mad that I felt like swinging at her. Then I suddenly remembered what you had said about difference of opinions, so I said, "Okay, we disagree. You have your opinion and I have mine. I'm sorry I got so angry about it." She

Tonya Koozer

calmed down and apologized too. I said, "You know, Brandy, we can still be friends, even if we disagree." She was surprised, and then we started apologizing to each other again.

Just by showing respect for Brandy's opinion, Simone salvaged their friendship. Simone could have avoided the first part of the argument, however, if she had calmly asked Brandy to explain what she meant. After listening to Brandy's entire line of reasoning, Simone could have asked her, "Did you ever look at it this way?" and then explain her opinion. Then, if Brandy still didn't agree, she could have ended up by saying, "You have your opinion, I have mine."

When you think about it, it really isn't necessary for our friends, relatives, and acquaintances to agree with us. Life would be boring if everyone thought exactly the way we do. It's really fine to disagree.

Here are some charts that will help you to use the information discussed in this chapter. By doing the exercises, you will apply the things you learned in the chapter to your own life-situation, and you will see your life begin to change for the better.

––––––––––––––

Make a list of your experiences in telling someone, "You're wrong."

Person	Statement	Results
Example: My brother.	"Your haircut makes you look older" (he said it). I said, "You're wrong; it makes me look younger."	We started to argue. He said I was blind.
1.		
2.		
3.		
4.		

Now go back to your list above and change your statement to one that would have avoided a fight.

Example: My brother.	"Yes. I see what you mean. From some angles I do look older, but a few people say I look younger. What do you think?"	My brother may say, "I see your point."
1.		
2.		
3.		
4.		

16

It's My Fault

When is the last time you did something wrong and got caught? Not long ago, I'll bet. And when you found yourself in this position, what did you do? I'll bet you immediately began to make excuses for yourself. You did the natural thing, but you made a mistake. The more you defend yourself, the more people break down those defenses and place the blame on you.

So what should you do if you are caught in a situation when you are dead wrong and you know it? Simple. Accuse yourself. Begin immediately attacking yourself. "How could I be so stupid. There's no excuse for my behavior. I deserve to be punished." When you do this, the person who was originally attacking you will soften and will begin to make your excuses for you. "Oh, it's not all that bad," the person will say. "We all make mistakes. Don't be so hard on yourself."

The psychology behind this reaction is easy to understand. Think of two fighters in a boxing ring. In order to fight, the opponents must be on opposite sides of the ring. So it is in a controversy. You make excuses. Your opponent accuses you. But if you accuse yourself, your opponent excuses you.

You will be delighted to see precisely how this works. "Hmm . . . neat trick. I can go around doing whatever I want and all I have to do is blame myself and I'll get away with it." No. Not at all. What I'm presenting to you is a way to get out of trouble by admitting your mistakes. If you're already in trouble, why not use psychology to get out of it the best way you can. You are in fact admitting your own guilt instead of denying it and trying to make excuses for yourself. The overall effect of this is that you will seem to be less arrogant. So let it be clear, you're not making a joke out of doing whatever you please and then worming your way out of it. You're merely learning to be honest about your blunders and in the process you will find that the blunder does not cause you more trouble than it should.

I asked some high school students to try the method out on parents, co-workers, and friends. They were suprised to see how simply it works.

Phillipe had this experience with his father.

When I came home from school my father had left a note on the table. He told me to take the dog downstairs. It was a beautiful day and I wanted to hang out, so I ignored the note and went downstairs for a while. After a while, I forgot about the dog. When I was going upstairs, I remembered about the dog and I was expecting my father to yell at me. When I saw him he looked very angry. My aunt had told him that I didn't take the dog down. He said very angrily, "Did you get my note?" I said, "I'm sorry, Daddy. I always do this to you. I know I should take the dog down because I know how tired you are when you come home from work. I'm such an ignorant son." When I said that, it took all the fight out of him. He said, "I forgive you. It was a beautiful day and you just wanted to enjoy it." By the way, he ended up taking the dog downstairs, even though I asked him to please let me do it.

Phillipe never bargained for not having to take the dog down at all, but his use of psychology worked so well that he got that as a bonus.

Lillian, who usually has endless arguments with her mother, had this experience.

I started eating ice cream in a plate in the living room. My mother hates it when we leave cups and plates all around the living room. When I was finished eating the ice cream, I forgot about the plate. She saw it and asked, "Who left this plate on the table?" She asked my brothers and sisters and then I remembered it was me. But before I could make an excuse, I thought, "Let me blame myself and see what happens." So I admitted I did it, and before she could open her mouth I said, "I'm sorry, Mom, I was wrong. I know you told me a hundred times not to leave plates in the living room. I don't know what's wrong with me. I'm so stupid." She said, "Don't worry, honey. It's okay. I forgive you. I understand. But don't call yourself stupid, because you're not, you simply forgot." I know if I hadn't done that she would have been really furious and would have yelled at me. I could not believe how it worked.

Ray had an opportunity to try this idea at work.

I work at this supermarket and when you go in you have to walk by a security guard. You're supposed to show your I.D. whenever you go in, but I didn't feel like taking it out, so I tried to go right past him. He wouldn't let me pass. He asked me my name and I told him. Then I got angry because I thought he should have recognized me. Anyway, he made me wait until the manager came out. Later I felt funny, so I decided to admit that I was wrong. I went over to him and said, "I was wrong. I should have had my I.D. out. I'm sorry for giving you a hard time." He said, "Well, I'm sorry I called the manager on you." Then he said, "No hard feelings," and we shook hands. Now we say hello to each other and he never asks for my I.D.

By not being too proud to apologize and by admitting that he was wrong, Ray made peace with a man he has to deal with every day. In this way he made his daily life easier and more pleasant. Isn't it better to have friends all around rather than enemies?

Admitting you're wrong can be important with friends too. You could have a serious argument and lose a friend for life. Why? You never believe you could make it right again. But why not trying admitting you were wrong?

Here's what happened to Sally.

One day this guy was talking to me and I knew he was going out with another girl, because she's my best friend's cousin. So like a dope, I went and told the girl that her boyfriend tried to make a pass at me. Then she went back and questioned him. The next day when I saw him he didn't even look at me. So I said, "Hey, listen, Van, I understand how you feel. What I did was wrong. I was so damn stupid about it, but I'm really sorry. If you don't even look at me

I can understand." Then he looked at me real seriously and said, "It's okay. I understand. Let's just forget the whole thing." Now we are good friends. I was happy with the results. There was a time when I could never admit I was wrong and feel good about it, but now I see that if you do, you come out winning in the end.

Sally saved her friendship by facing up to her mistake. As you can see, the approach is almost irresistible.

Lauretta had an argument with a friend, and instead of waiting days to make up with her, she settled the issue on the spot by taking part of the blame. Here's what happened.

I got mad at a friend and really told her off. I had been in a bad mood so I picked a fight with her. After that I could see that I had hurt her feelings and began to feel guilty. I waited a few minutes to think of how to apologize, and then I said, "I'm sorry. I was wrong to curse at you. There was no excuse for it. The whole argument was my fault. I'm upset about my boyfriend so I took it out on you." She said, "Oh, it's all right. I understand. I do the same thing myself sometimes," and she started to smile again. I felt much better.

Isn't it better to apologize and admit that you were wrong than to feel bad about it all day long? It takes nerve to admit you're wrong, but in the end people will respect you more and you'll feel much better about yourself. Most of the time the person will forgive you. People are really softhearted, but they're afraid to show it. If you break the ice, you'll see amazing things happen.

Opportunities to admit you're wrong come up all the time, at home, at school, and at work. Be alert and see what you can do to change the way things ordinarily turn out in a situation when you are "dead wrong."

Here are some charts that will help you to use the information discussed in this chapter. By doing the exercises, you will apply the things you learned in the chapter to your own life-situation, and you will see your life begin to change for the better.

Make a list of the times you accuse rather than defend yourself. Record the results.

Offense	Accuser	They Said	I Said	Results
Example: Forgot to go to the store.	My mother.	"How could you?"	"I must be in another world."	She said, "Okay, go later."
1.				
2.				
3.				
4.				
5.				
6.				
7.				
8.				
9.				
10.				

17

I'm Feeling Good

Did you ever say to yourself, "I don't need anybody. I can make it by myself?" Sure. Up to a point, people *can* make it by themselves. But what would life be like if no one was around to help you?

People need people. More specifically, people need you. Your power to bring joy to others is endless. You can make people so happy that they won't know what to do first, kiss you, thank you, or just jump for joy. Strangely enough, when you do this for someone else, you yourself experience a strange kind of joy, a joy that must be experienced to be understood.

Think, for example, how your mother would feel if you surprised her by cleaning the house before she got home from work. Tara did it and here's what happened.

One day my mother wasn't home so I decided to cook. I made a very good dinner and I cleaned up the entire house. When my mother got home, all tired, she couldn't believe her eyes. When she saw the dinner, she came over to me, gave me a big hug, and said, "You're so thoughtful. I love you." She had tears in her eyes.

There are many opportunities to make people happy by doing something for them. You could surprise your boy-friend or girl friend with a small gift, or visit a sick relative in the hospital, or call someone just to find out how they are. You have no idea how much little things like that mean to people. They'll never forget you for it.

When you go out of your way to do a good deed, positive things happen. You get a wonderful feeling about yourself, and the person you do the favor for usually starts treating you with more respect and affection. Victoria had this experience.

Yesterday I helped this man when no one else did. The old man, a bum, had fallen in the street, and everyone just laughed at him. But I felt sorry for him, so I went over and helped him to get up. No one expected me to help him, but I did. After I had helped him I felt good. I really can't explain it, but I felt great.

Here's what happened to Lisa when she was generous.

Yesterday I went with my cousin to look for a job. On the way back we stopped at a restaurant. While we were waiting for our food we noticed this guy who didn't have enough money to pay. He looked embarrassed, and he was going through his pockets looking for money. I thought about giving him the money he needed, but then I didn't want to get involved. Then I decided to be generous. I got my wallet and took out a dollar and gave it to him. At first he didn't want to take it but I said, "Listen, don't worry about it. Some day I might need help and someone will help me out." Then he smiled, took the money, and thanked me. When he got the change he tried to give it back to me but I told him to keep it. He was smiling and thanking me, and he looked embarrassed. I felt so good that I didn't know what to say to my cousin when we were eating lunch. My cousin said, "I guess you must feel real good." I said, "Yes. I feel great."

Lisa put herself in the young man's place. She imagined what it would be like if she needed the change. She overcame her laziness and got involved. She had the power to help another person in trouble and she used it. Dozens of other people must have heard him say he didn't have enough money, but it was Lisa who took action.

Lisa, like all of us, was tempted not to "get involved." But she overcame that feeling. That's the purpose of this book: to point out that we can do what is right and necessary to make something wonderful happen in life. It's like magic. It's like creating your own life, your own destiny.

Lavon was generous and he became highly respected by his friends. He was, in fact, given more love and respect than before, not that he had this in mind when he did a good deed.

I have this friend named Reggie. He was opening this little clubhouse and he asked me if I wanted to check it out. The house looked okay, but it didn't have much furniture. I remembered that my father had put these two small coffee tables in the basement. So I said, "You want to take a walk with me over to my house and I'll ask my father if he needs those coffee tables he put in the basement?" So we went to my house and my father said I could have them. We got the tables and brought them to the clubhouse. I helped Reggie shine them up. He said, "Man, I ain't gonna be letting everybody up here, but you can come up anytime you want to."

Why did Lavon get the invitation to Reggie's private clubhouse? Evidently Lavon's generosity had the inevitable effect of making Reggie want to be generous with him and to give him special treatment.

Paulette, who used to fight with her sister about her record collection, had this experience.

One day I was in the record shop and I saw this record that my older sister always talked about getting. I had a little extra money so I decided to buy it for her. When I gave it to her, she thought I wanted her to pay me for it. When I told her it was a gift, she didn't know how to react. She was so happy she started playing the record immediately. After that, she said I could use her records anytime I wanted to. Before that she used to yell at me whenever I touched her records.

Paulette didn't get the record for her sister with the goal of being allowed to use her sister's records anytime. But the effect was still the same. Her sister responded to Paulette's generosity, and became more generous herself. Generosity is contagious. It really is. It's up to you to start the trend. It really isn't a new idea. The Bible said it a long time ago. "Give and it shall be given unto you."

Here are some charts that will help you to use the information discussed in this chapter. By doing the exercises, you will apply the things you learned in the chapter to your own life-situation, and you will see your life begin to change for the better.

———————————

Keep a record of your generosity. Record the results.

Person	What I Did	Results
Example: Mother.	Sent her flowers for no special occasion.	She bragged to everyone about it and kept telling me how happy she is.
1.		
2.		
3.		
4.		
5.		
6.		
7.		
8.		
9.		
10.		

18

I Dare You

You're the one, the one who will decide what happens to you. I dare you to go out there and get exactly what you want out of life. I dare you to accept life's challenges no matter how difficult or even dangerous they may be.

I dare you to do the thing that you fear the most.

I dare you to take what Robert Frost, the renowned poet, called "The Road Not Taken." He said,

> Two roads diverged in a wood, and I—
> I took the one less traveled by,
> And that has made all the difference.

Your "road not taken" could be the road to becoming a professional baseball player. It could be the road to college.

It could be any difficult or daring road that you are afraid of at the time. But think of it. If you don't take that more difficult road, that road less traveled, later on in life you will know that something is missing. But you will never know what could have been.

Those who dare to take the road less traveled see "all the difference" in their lives. I know many adults who look back at their lives and can point to a particular time when they should have tried for something in their younger days. I know a man who didn't become a professional football player because the girl he wanted to marry said she wouldn't marry him if he did. He ended up divorcing her a few years later and now he is working at a job he hates, talking about how he "could have" become a pro.

Muhammad Ali, on the other hand, took the "road not taken." He and everyone else now knows what "all the difference" made in his life. There was a time when he was very poor, so poor that he had to wait until other fighters were finished fighting in the gym so that he could borrow their headgear or boxing trunks. He could have quit. He could have said, "I'm too poor. Too many things are against me." But he didn't. He went on and became world champion. If he didn't dare to take a difficult road, I wouldn't be writing about him now.

What about you? Will someone be writing about you years from now because you dared to take the road not taken?

The road not taken. I dare you to take it. Graduate from high school even though it's difficult. Go to college. Try for that difficult job. Get what you want out of life.

Look at the sky. See how big it is? That's your limit—the sky.

The road not taken. I dare you to take it.

– BIBLIOGRAPHY –

Bradley, David G. *Circles of Faith*. New York: Abingdon
　　　Press, 1966.
　A simple presentation of each of the five major religions.

Bristol, Claude M. *The Magic of Believing*. New York:
　　　Pocket Books, 1948.
　A classic that challenges the reader to obtain any and every
goal ever desired, with clear-cut methods on exactly how to
go about it.

Buscaglia, Leo, Ph.D. *Living, Loving & Learning*. New
　　　York: Holt, Rinehart and Winston, 1982.
　Insightful discussions on coping with various emotions and
life situations.

Campbell, David. *If You Don't Know Where You're Going,*

You'll Probably End Up Somewhere Else. Niles,
    Illinois: Argus Communications, 1974.
This book gives the reader information on exactly how to
set up his or her life so that success is almost inevitable.

Collier, James Lincoln. *The Hard Life of the Teenager*.
    New York: Four Winds Press, 1972.
  Gives the teenager insight into his feelings about parents,
sex, and social position. Helps a teenager to understand his or
her parents.

Fitzgerald, Dr. Ernest A. *How to Be a Successful Failure*.
    New York: Atheneum, 1978.
Points out that success is making the most and the best of
what you have. Inspirational, excellent psychology. Encourages individuality and success.

The Good News Bible. American Bible Society.
A modern translation of the Bible. Easy reading for young
adults.

Kiev, Ari, M.D. *Riding Through the Downers, Hassles,
    Snags and Funks*. New York: E. P. Dutton, 1980.
Deals very well with the problem of depression and thoughts
of suicide. Tells how to get out of depression and to use negative
experiences to improve.

Lorayne, Harry, and Lucas, Jerry. *The Memory Book*. New
    York: Ballantine Books, 1974.
A book filled with ways to improve your ability to remember
names, faces, etc.

Maltz, Maxwell, M.D., F.I.C.S. *Psychocybernetics*. New
    York: Pocket Books, 1960.
An excellent classic on how to change one's self-image from
negative to positive, and how to achieve one's deepest desires.

McGough, Elizabeth. *Who Are You? A Teen-Ager's Guide*

to Self-Understanding. New York: William Morrow, 1977.

This book gives the teenager deep insight into his relationship with parents.

Miller, Gordon Porter. *Life Choices*. New York: T. Y. Crowell, 1978.

This is a book that teaches the individual to calmly, logically, and analytically consider all alternatives when making decisions.

Muhammad Ali. *The Greatest*. New York: Random House, 1975.

The life story of Muhammad Ali, written by the man himself. Shows how, in spite of incredible odds, a person can do the "impossible."

Peale, Norman Vincent. *You Can if You Think You Can*. Englewood Cliffs, N. J.: Prentice-Hall, 1975.

Challenges the young person to make the most of life and to overcome obstacles. Emphasizes relentless determination and positive thinking. Many inspiring success stories.

Watts, Alan. *God*. Millbrae, California: Celestial Arts, 1974.

An insightful, philosophical approach to the concept of God and religious ideas. Very brief and to the point.

Warner, Lucille and Reit, Ann. *Your A to Z Super-Personality Quiz*. New York: Scholastic Books, 1977.

An A-Z personality quiz, giving the reader a chance to see if he or she is, for example, "jealous." Discusses various personality quirks and how to overcome them. Excellent book for teenagers.

–Index–

– ABOUT THE AUTHOR –

Joyce Vedral has a Ph.D. in English Literature, teaches at Julia Richman High School, and is an adjunct assistant associate professor at Pace University, writes for *Muscle and Fitness Magazine*, and is the author of SUPER CUT and HARD BODIES.

Ms. Vedral has studied Jiu-jitsu, Judo, and Go-Ju Karate and is a brown belt in Judo. She has also won many bodybuilding competitions. In addition, she has climbed Mt. Kenya in East Africa and the Grand Tetons.

Joyce was raised in the Bronx in an area usually termed, "the ghetto." She refuses to accept defeat and has proved it by her life. She dares you to do exactly what you want with your life, starting TODAY.

HELP!

For parents who want to raise their children better... and for the adults those children will become.

Tonya Koozer